MW01611443

LEADERSHIP BY

BECOME THE LEADER YOU
WERE CREATED TO BE

Jeremy Stalnecker

Foreword By Dan Dow

"Leaders aren't born, they are made. And they are made just like anything else, through hard work. And that's the price we'll have to pay to achieve that goal, or any goal."

- Vince Lombardi

What others are saying about *Leadership By Design*

"All of us have areas in which we must lead. But many fail to do so because of a faulty understanding of leadership, for leading is not about what you do, it's about who you are. Whether you are a leader who has lost his way or someone who has yet to begin, Leadership By Design will give you the insight and direction you need to lead others the way God intended."

David Barton
"America's Historian"
Founder & President of WallBuilders
New York Times Best-Selling Author, the Jefferson Lies

"What would our world look like today if leaders understood the ultimate goal of leadership? There have been hundreds of "how to" leadership books written to help you attain wealth and power. Leadership by Design captures the very essence of leadership if your goal is to enrich the lives of those you lead. It is a must read for those who want to leave a legacy worth following."

Colonel Bill Coate
USMC, Retired
Author-You, The Last Best Hope To Restore Our Nation

"Jeremy Stalnecker has led in just about every conceivable situation – combat, family, ministry, and everything in-between! What he shares with us in "Leadership By Design" has been learned and then lived out in the laboratory of real life experiences. Prepare to learn not only "what" to do, but to understand "why" it needs to be done."

Pastor Stephen Chappell
Pastor, Coastline Baptist Church
Author

Leadership By Design

© 2017 All Rights Reserved
Jeremy M. Stalnecker

Limit of Liability/Disclaimer of Warranty: While the publisher and authors have used their best efforts in preparing this book, they make no representations or warranties with respect to the accuracy and completeness of the contents of this book and specifically disclaim any implied warranties of merchantability or fitness for a particular purpose. No warranty may be created or extended by sales representatives or written sales materials. The advice and strategies contained herein may not be suitable for your situation. The author and publisher are not engaged in rendering professional, legal or medical services, and you should consult a professional where appropriate. The authors and publisher shall not be liable for any loss of profit, nor any personal or commercial damages, including but not limited to special, incidental, consequential, or other damages.

All Scriptures quotations are taken from the King James Version.

All rights reserved. No part of this book may be reproduced or transmitted in any form or by any means except as permitted under Section 107 or 108 of the 1976 United States Copyright Act and with written permission from the author. All materials are legal property of Jeremy M. Stalnecker. Unauthorized duplication is strictly forbidden and punishable to the maximum extent under applicable law.

ISBN: 978-0-9863193-3-4 Leadership by Design Paperback

Edited by: Kate Lehman
Cover Design by: Nash Hagen
Published by: *Making Life Better Publishing*
Learn more information about the author at:
www.LeadershipByDesignBook.com

To Susanne, my hero.

CONTENTS

Acknowledgements

For as long as I can remember I have wanted to write a book. I have always appreciated the written word and the wisdom that it can communicate when employed by the artists that we call authors. Worlds can be created, wisdom can be dispensed and the deep truths of scripture can be made clear. I have so much respect for those that write, in fact, that every time I have thought about writing a book of my own I have quickly dismissed the thought as the overwhelming wave of inadequacy would come over me. With so much that has been written, why would anyone want to read something from me? And then, just as I would start to believe that maybe I could put together some words that may be of interest to someone, the daunting task of producing a book would push me back to the familiar place of procrastination-someday. Thankfully, writing and producing a book does not have to be a solo endeavor. There are those who encourage, those who critique, and those who help to create.

While it would be impossible to mention everyone by name, I am fully, and humbly, aware that this book would not have been completed without a great deal of help from some great people. For those that read and helped me to refine the thoughts in early drafts, thank you. Thank you to John Mizerak and Making Life Better Publishing for keeping me on task and pulling all the production pieces together. To Kate Lehman for your helpful and thoughtful editing. To the many men and women that I have been blessed to know, serve with, and learn from that have taught me the essence of leadership and what it truly means to serve others. To the men of the Mighty Oaks Foundation: I have learned more from you than you will ever know.

And to the one who is worthy of all honor:

Now unto him that is able to do exceeding abundantly above all that we ask or think, according to the power that worketh in us, Unto him be glory in the church by Christ Jesus throughout all ages, world without end. Amen (Ephesians 3:20-21)

Thank you.

Foreword

One of my favorite quotes that illustrates the need for courageous leadership is one that has often been attributed to British statesman Edmund Burke, "*[t]he only thing necessary for the triumph of evil is for good men to do nothing*." Whether Burke said it or not, the words ring solidly true. A leader recognizes that he must step up and *do something* so that he or his organization is not defeated.

If a ship sails without a Captain, it will quickly stray off course. If a business loses its Chief Executive, it will soon begin to lose its effectiveness. If a winning football team loses its coach or its star player, it will likely start losing its games. We can agree that leadership is essential to the long-term success of any type of organization.

While we recognize the need for leadership, it often tends to be a commodity that we look for other people to deliver. We tell ourselves that someone else will step up and take the reins. Or, we conclude that we are not the best one for the job. We don't believe that we have what it takes to lead. When no one is willing to step up and lead, catastrophe can and will likely strike. So, where can we find the leaders that we need to take us where we need to be? How do we gain the necessary ingredients to become a leader?

Within the pages of this book, Jeremy Stalnecker explains that leaders are developed over time by intentionally becoming the men and women they were created to be. He goes on to reveal a perfect blueprint for becoming an effective leader and introduces the reader to the architect who made the blueprint for effective leadership.

If you are struggling to find purpose in your life; if you lack the motivation to step up and lead in your family, career, or organization; or if you don't believe that you have what it takes to lead, this book will help you discover your God-given purpose and will provide a solid roadmap to becoming an effective leader.

If you're tired of sitting on the sidelines and waiting for others to *do something* so that evil does not triumph, I challenge you to read this book with a commitment to step up and become the leader you were created to be so that you can fulfill your purpose to *take others from where they are to where they need to be.*

Dan Dow

District Attorney
County of San Luis Obispo, California
Staff Judge Advocate, United States Army
Bronze Star Recipient

Introduction

Writing a book on leadership is a little bit like writing a book on religion or philosophy; there are thousands of books that have been written over thousands of years from thousands of perspectives. Politicians and generals have written leadership books, as well as teachers, Christian leaders, and some of the world's greatest thinkers. There are "how to" books dealing with the practical steps of organizational leadership and books outlining failures in leadership that can serve as lessons learned. So, with all that has been written on this topic, the natural questions that a reader should ask are, *"Why is another book on this topic needed, and what qualifies you to write it?"* These are both fair questions that need to be answered.

"Why does another book on this topic need to be written?"

As a parent of four children, I've given what I believe to be sound advice based on years of personal experience to my kids many times over the years. Often, however, this advice is quietly dismissed or even angrily rejected as ill-informed or out of touch. It seems that every child lives with the consistent belief that their parents have always been adults. What is amazing to me, though, is that the same advice given by someone else can be considered sheer genius. Apparently, everyone outside of my home is more qualified to give advice than me, and sometimes the advice given can only be trusted if it comes from someone with a different last name! While many can relate to similar situations and the frustration they bring (although I am glad that my kids have received some great advice from others), there is just something in our human nature that makes an outside perspective more relevant.

While I am confident that leadership is something that's been discussed since the time of Adam and Eve (I am sure this came up after the whole serpent and fruit incident), I hope to provide a different perspective on this very important topic. This is not a book that will outline specific leadership techniques or provide lists dealing with how to lead in the home, church, or workplace. My goal is to provide a **philosophy of leadership** and leadership development around which specific techniques can be built. We all have different goals when it comes to either developing our own leadership or developing those around us. What does not change, however, is the philosophy or foundation upon which that development should take place. My goal is to provide a fresh look at the fundamental principles that need to be present in the life of every leader.

"What qualifies you to write this book?"

I have had the privilege throughout my life of observing and participating in leadership from several different perspectives. I haven't always gotten it right, but I have spent most of my life around those who have. I grew up in a home with a mom and dad that both understand leadership in a very fundamental way. They have lived their lives leading themselves and those around them well and have provided an example of the servant leadership about which so much has been written. I don't remember ever having a conversation with my parents about leading, per se, but the example of their lives has been an ongoing conversation spoken without words.

In college I was challenged by instructors who understood leadership and were more interested in their students' grasp of how to lead than they were in many of the more academic pursuits. From there I went into the Marine Corps, perhaps the finest leadership school in the world. I was taught many things as a young officer, but the one thing ever present was the belief that in peacetime or war the willingness and ability to lead makes everything else possible. I had the amazing opportunity to put these lessons to use as I led an infantry platoon during the initial invasion into Iraq. There is no more dynamic environment for leadership than the combat environment, and I saw firsthand, from Kuwait to Baghdad and back again, the leadership principles that really matter. The leaders I had the honor of following are men who are leading our military and our country today because of their innate grasp of these principles.

In my first job after leaving the Marine Corps, I learned what ministry leadership looks like and the sacrifices that need to be made to both follow a calling and lead those that often do not want to be led. My pastor patiently mentored and trained me so that I would be able to lead in this new and often overwhelming capacity. When I moved on to become the senior pastor of a church in the San Francisco Bay Area, several men graciously and patiently walked me through the twists and turns of pastoral life. This was a very different leadership environment, but one that taught me how to apply the other lessons I have learned to lead individuals and families forward in their own lives.

At each stage of my life God has placed me around leaders who have taught and trained and cared for me while equipping me to lead in capacities well beyond my own ability. In a very real way I believe that I have a responsibility to those who have not had the same opportunities as me to share the gift that I have been given.

Perhaps the thing that most strongly qualifies me to write a book like this one, though, is not my personal leadership growth curve or the examples of leadership that I have had the privilege of observing. For the last several years I have had the enormous privilege of being a part of the Mighty Oaks Foundation and the Mighty Oaks Warrior Programs. I have served within the organization in several capacities and now am blessed to serve as Executive Director of this ministry.

Mighty Oaks Warrior Programs exists to help the men and women who have served or are currently serving our country to re-engage with life outside the military so they can live in alignment with who they were created to be. Put simply, we work to help those who have lost their way to regain their purpose and live their lives according to it. Not surprisingly, when an individual is living aligned to their purpose, everything in their life changes. Their personal outlook, relational life, and interaction with the rest of the world is meaningful and fulfilling because they are doing what they were created to do. Many of these men and women have been clinically diagnosed with Post Traumatic Stress Disorder (PTSD) from either their combat experience or other life traumas. Many have been hospitalized for attempted self-harm or simply because they lack the emotional ability to live a meaningful life. Those who attend the programs offered by Mighty Oaks are often at the end of their road with nowhere to turn.

What is amazing about this, at least from my perspective, is that unlike many other areas in our society, one of the things these men and women have in common is that they have all been taught leadership and, in one capacity or another, have been the one leading! We are working to take broken leaders and get them back into the game, to provide a framework around which those who have been warriors and leaders in another life can embrace the purpose for which they were created once again. With thousands of students completing our programs and tens of thousands participating in our ongoing resiliency events, we've had the opportunity again and again to watch this happen.

It is my firmly held belief, based on observing broken men and women turn the mess of their lives into a message that aligns with their purpose, that we have all been created to lead! Those who are not leading have simply lost their way or have never been challenged to accept a life that is bigger than simply getting by. Leadership will look different for everyone. Some will lead themselves well and others will lead companies and countries. The "what" is not so important. It is living within the framework of your design that makes all the difference.

So, whether you are a leader who has fallen or simply stopped leading because of the circumstances of life, or someone who has seen leadership as something other people do, let me make the premise of this book clear: If you are not leading in some capacity according to your unique talents, abilities, and opportunities, you are not living the life you were created to live. We were designed from the moment of creation to lead others in a way that helps them get to the place they need to go. This is not something that we do; it is who we are! Decide before you turn the next page that you will lead according to the principles that have been life changing for thousands of people just like you. Decide that you will embrace the philosophy of *leadership by design.*

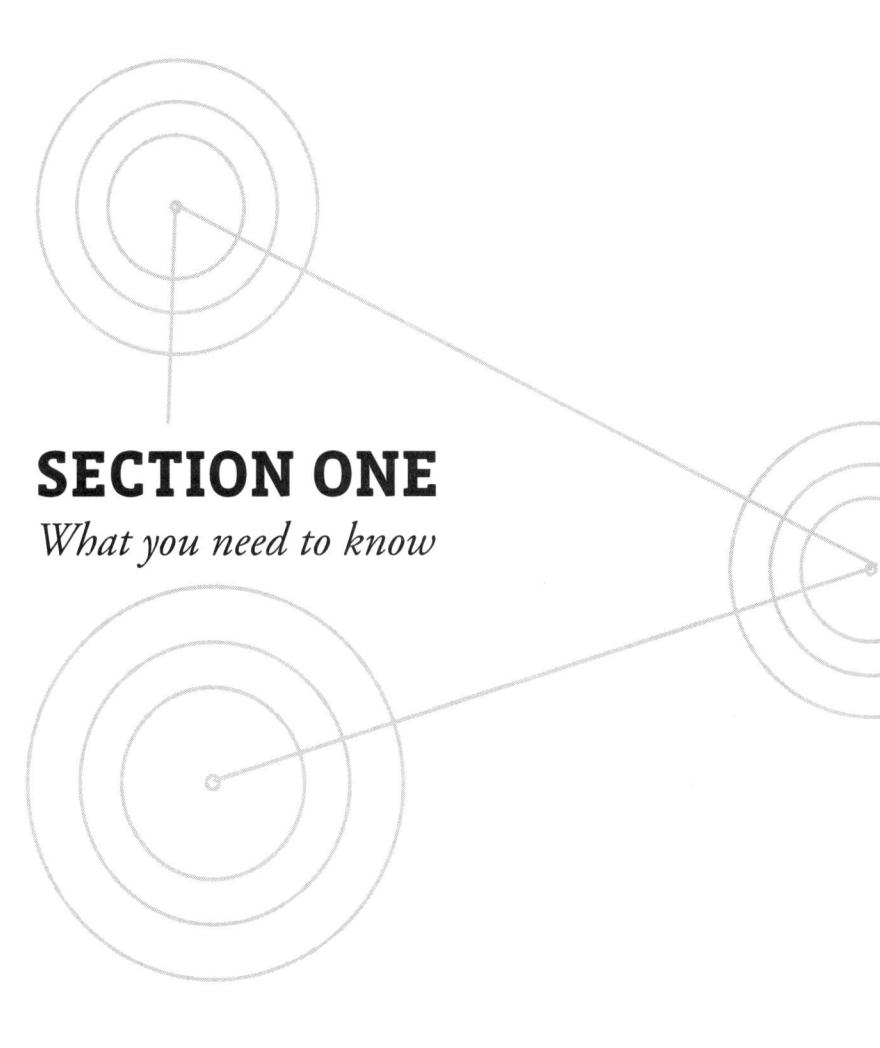

SECTION ONE

What you need to know

Chapter 1

A Leadership Definition

You can't hit a target you cannot see,
and you cannot see a target you do not have.[1]

Any discussion of leadership needs to begin with a definition. How leadership is defined changes from one person to the next based on life experience, background, education, and culture. What looks like leadership to one person can look like a dictatorship to another. Some would say that leaders are always "type A," while others believe in a more passive approach. In many ways, this is why learning to lead or regaining the ability to lead is so difficult. We are trying to hit a target that we can name but cannot see.

It is amazing how often history will illustrate truths that can help us today. This story from World War II perfectly shows the importance of identifying your target. Following the invasion of Normandy in 1944, a plan, codenamed "Operation Cobra," was developed to finally break the back of the German army. The goal was to give the Allied forces the opportunity they needed to break German defenses and regain control of France and the rest of Europe. While the D-Day invasion was considered a success, more needed to be done to finally drive the German army out.

Although this massive Allied operation would be a key victory against the Axis Powers, it did not start out that way. Due to weather-related visibility issues, the bombers that would engage German troops had to start their attack a day later than scheduled. On July 25, more than 5,000 bombers began to engage key enemy targets. Unfortunately, in what was otherwise a resounding success, the 1,800 bombers from the Eighth Air Force mistakenly killed 111 Allied Soldiers and wounded 490 others. Among those killed was Lieutenant General Wesley McNair, who became the highest-ranking U.S. soldier to be killed while fighting in Europe.

While we understand that things like this have probably happened in every war, "friendly fire" incidents always beg the question, *"Why?"* Sadly, this was the second time in two days an incident like this had taken place. On July 24, the day before the full-scale bombardment, limited engagement by bombers resulted in the deaths of more than 25 Americans with 130 more wounded. Poor visibility made it impossible for the bombers to know whom they were hitting. They couldn't see the right target, so they hit the wrong one!

The next day, when visibility returned, the Eighth Air Force engaged the wrong target again because they were in the wrong place. Confusion regarding the location of friendly ground troops caused the pilots to think they were killing the enemy when they were engaging their own troops.[2] It is impossible to know how many soldiers have been killed by their own troops since the beginning of warfare, but it's a tragedy when we consider how often events like this could have been avoided if the target had been clear.

Here is the point put as simply as I know how: it is impossible to hit the target if we cannot see it! We may be working hard and doing our best, but a goal that is not clearly defined will never be achieved. In a massive military operation like the one described above, I cannot help but think of the many resources that were invested—time, materials, coordination between countries, and years of training for those who would carry it out. I imagine that for the men involved there was even a sense of accomplishment immediately following their actions. But then they found out who they had dropped bombs on! The resources, time and energy were all wasted simply because the target was not clear.

And so it is in life. Many will come to the end of their lives exhausted and disillusioned because even though they invested everything they had into everything they did, they accomplished very little since they never defined their goal. For leaders, the lesson is the same. Until we have a clear definition, we cannot truly lead. I believe this is often the reason discouraged leaders quit and others decide it would be easier to never start. If we don't settle on a clear definition of leadership, it is impossible to know if the goal has been accomplished.

So, how do we define leadership?

Put simply, leadership is taking someone from where they are to where they need to be.

This is not hard to understand, but it runs contrary to much of what we've been taught about leadership. Often what is defined as leadership is nothing more than a plan to get people to do what you want them to do. That is a lot more manipulation than it is leadership. Unfortunately, the ability to get people to help you accomplish your goals has become the criteria by which we determine whether someone is really a leader.

When we begin to view leadership based on the definition given above, however, everything changes. Our approach toward others, the view that we have of ourselves, and the goals that we pursue in our relationships will all be different when we realize that leading is not about getting what we want from others, but rather helping others get what they need most. It's about bringing clarity to situations that are unclear and providing the necessary resources to accomplish the task at hand. It is investing in those around you so that they can be what they were created to be instead of using them to help you accomplish your own goals.

The Application

There are many situations in which this shift in focus may resonate, but let me use two to illustrate.

In the Home

First, consider this definition of leadership in the context of a family. One of the major frustrations that parents and spouses have is getting those in their family to do what they want them to do. Many parents give up because they simply cannot get their kids to obey. You send the kids to their room to clean and hope that when you check on them something will be done. Disappointed again. I am always amazed when things look worse after the kids get done cleaning than they did before.

While parents are resilient and disappointment is just a part of this grand adventure of raising children, many parents decide to let the kids do what they want to instead of following the rules or finishing their chores. After all, it's better than locking them in the backyard, and dropping them off on the side of the road is illegal! I used to judge parents who quit trying to get their kids to obey. Now I envy them.

Even with well-behaved children things can be hard. I've had many conversations with husbands and fathers who are frustrated because they cannot get their families to do what they want them to do. They set a course for the family that they, the fathers, believe will provide the most fulfillment but cannot get the rest of the family to go along. Every time I have this conversation, it is delivered with a "you wouldn't understand" tone. I always laugh a little inside because it would be embarrassing to start crying when I'm trying to help someone. I can barely rally my family to get in the car, let alone on the same page regarding our collective future. It can be a real struggle.

The problem is when men who should be the leaders and providers in their homes conclude that it just isn't worth the trouble and throw in the proverbial leadership towel. Add to that stories of parents who will not let their children go, or who find their identity in their kids and decide that it's best to let them set the agenda, and it's no wonder our homes are often places of frustration and disappointment instead of joy and fulfillment. Despite what many think about their home, though, the problem in most of these situations is a misunderstanding of leadership.

Imagine if spouses and parents started to view leadership in the home based on the simple definition at the beginning of this chapter. *Leadership is taking someone from where they are to where they need to be.* Our relationship with our children would be different. Now I'm not trying to get them to obey the rules because that's what I want them to do or because well-behaved children make me feel good about myself. I begin to view the jobs I give them and the expectations I set for them in terms of them. These are my children, and I have a responsibility to get them ready for life. I want them to be mature, well-adjusted adults, and I need to invest in them now so they can function on their own when they leave my home. It's not about getting what I want out of them, but about taking them from where they are to where they need to be.

This doesn't mean that things are going to get easier or that they are going to jump on board because you explain that you're preparing them for their future. It does, however, provide focus and clarity about the things you want them to do and the expectations you have. It also helps you when you have those "why am I doing this" moments.

How does this apply to the weary leaders of the home? Too often we believe that leading our homes is getting the family to do what we want them to do instead of helping them to do what they need to do. This is a subtle difference, but it changes the way we set priorities and evaluate the direction in which we are traveling as a family. When the goal is to make decisions and provide resources that will move your family from where they are to where they need to be, the pressure on you lifts—now the goal is to do what is best for everyone else. You lead and do what needs to be done, understanding that you cannot make anyone follow. You can only do what is best for them. Since this is no longer about you, doing what is best or right is the goal instead of using manipulation to get what you want.

In the Workplace

Unless you're self-employed, politics and manipulation are a consistent part of what you deal with in your workplace. That may even be a problem if you're self-employed. Who am I to judge! In some places this is the exception and in some it's the rule. Regardless, the desire to advance and be recognized for the work you do can be a powerful motivator when getting the people around you to do what you want them to do. Leadership in the workplace can often be nothing more than management by force. The tools of money and position are used to advance an agenda that is often very personal.

I do not believe as many do that companies exist for the employee. Companies exist to produce things and make money. When employees forget that, they become frustrated and even angry because they feel their company owes them something beyond the terms spelled out in their contract. The company does not. The employee is hired to help the company succeed. In the not-for-profit world, employees are hired to help the organization accomplish its stated objectives.

In the workplace, unfortunately, it is easy to forget why we were hired. Let's be honest, most people do not take a job because of the job. We work so we can get the resources needed take care of those for whom we're responsible. Kids like to eat and landlords like to get their rent checks, and providing either without a job is difficult. So we can find ourselves in an environment where leading means getting what we want from those we work with or those we work for.

What would happen if we took a different definition into the workplace? If we decided that even at our job leadership is *taking someone from where they are to where they need to be?* We need to understand that our job, regardless of our job description or title, is to help those around us succeed. If we are in charge we need to realize that helping those we lead accomplish their goals helps us accomplish ours. This not about being taken advantage of but about thinking in terms of those you lead instead of in terms of yourself. When those you lead succeed, so do you. If an employee is unwilling to work for someone who has his or her best interest in mind, then it may be time for the employee to leave the team.

Help others help themselves and move them from where they currently are to where they really need to be.

Perhaps the person you must lead is yourself. The principle still applies. Don't forget that your job is helping those in charge move from where they are to where they need to be. Don't let them violate the terms of your employment, and don't work for someone who tries. If your employer is doing what they said they would do, then do what you said you would do. Work to make them successful. You might be amazed at the progress you make in your own work situation when your goal is to "lead up" by helping the team to succeed.

Principle vs. Technique

Often, the definitions offered for leadership are not really definitions as much as techniques or methods used to lead. They are tied to jobs or personality types instead of the essence of leadership itself. And there is a major difference.

The confusion in this area is one of the reasons many people stop leading when they are no longer able to do some of the things they used to and why many never learn to lead at all. The work I'm involved in at the Mighty Oaks Foundation is unique for several reasons, but one reason in particular is that most of the people who attend our programs have previously demonstrated an ability and fortitude to lead. Dealing with those who have been in the military means that, at least on some level, they were taught leadership principles and had to use them to lead at least one other person. And yet, even though they've demonstrated leadership ability, they've come to a point in their life where they just don't want to do it anymore. They make this decision using a number of criteria, but a common theme is that they just can't do what they used to do. They were taught how to lead but can't follow those steps anymore. And since they can't do it that way, they decide they can't lead at all. When leadership is a technique, the ability to lead disappears as soon as the technique becomes obsolete.

If being a leader requires standing on a table and screaming orders, or, on the other hand, demands an intellect and personality that others cannot help but follow, then most people will never be able to lead. We make a mistake when we equate leadership ability with a particular type of person or feel that leadership is only required in specific situations. When we conclude that we cannot lead because we lack the personality, intellect, or influence of others, we limit our own ability to fulfill the purpose for which we were created. We were created to lead on some level, but we disqualify ourselves because we think that leadership is a "how" instead of a "what". We need a definition that guides what we do regardless of the situation. Techniques change based on circumstance and will look different from one person to the next. But the essence of leadership that holds those techniques up never changes.

A number of years ago, I heard an interview with Dr. Ben Carson. When the interviewer asked about his childhood and how he developed his well-known work ethic, he told the story of how his mother pushed him and his brother to do better in school. He said that every day when they got home, their single mom, exhausted from work, would ask to see their homework. Dr. Carson said that she would look it over carefully and circle the things she thought needed improvement. She was always pushing them to do better and to turn in the very best work they could. This heartwarming story took on a profound meaning when he told the interviewer that it wasn't until years later that he learned his mother couldn't even read. She looked at their papers and pushed them to be better because she knew that's where they needed to be. She led her kids despite her own circumstances and shortcomings in a way that allowed them to accomplish what they were placed on this earth to accomplish. Leadership has nothing to do with technique or ability and everything to do with leveraging what you have for the good of others.

Technique is important, but it doesn't define leadership. Leadership in the home will look very different than leadership on the battlefield if, instead of leading according to a style, we lead according to a principle. This definition, *taking someone from where they are to where they need to be,* can serve as that guiding principle.

A Leadership Example

The best example we can find of this philosophy being lived out is in the life of Jesus Christ. To my mind, one of the best leadership texts we have is found in the Bible in Philippians chapter 2. In a letter written by Paul the Apostle to a local church we find instructions on how people in the church should treat each other.

Paul begins chapter 2 by saying that love should bring unity instead of division to the congregation. He illustrates how people from different backgrounds can care for each other, using the life of Christ as an example. He talks about how Christ, being God in human flesh, never stopped being God while He was on earth. In fact, He never forgot that He was God or thought it inappropriate to be recognized as God. But, Paul tells the church, even though Jesus is God, He still allowed himself to be crucified so that He could pay the price for sin. You see, even though Jesus is God, the Creator of the universe and the Sustainer of life, He died for our sin, not because He needed to, but because we needed Him to! He did not do what was in His best interest—He did what was in ours. He took us from where we were, living in our own sin, to where we needed to be, eternally forgiven for that sin. Not everyone will accept the gift of forgiveness, but He did what was necessary so that those who want to actually can.

The leader is not a manipulator or dictator, but simply makes it possible for those he leads to move from where they are to where they need to be. On some level those who are led need to be willing, but as we see with Christ, the leader does the hard work of making the right decisions and the right steps possible. There is no leader greater than Christ, and we see in His example that philosophy or principle must guide our leadership decisions instead of technique.

From this example we see three important truths that will help us as we discuss this topic.

1. We were created for a purpose.

There was a moment in Jesus' ministry when He made His purpose on this earth clear to all of those around Him. He said in Luke 19:10, *"For the Son of Man is come to seek and to save that which was lost."* As we read the gospels and consider the brief period of time Jesus actually ministered, it's clear that those three years were extremely difficult. He was rejected, slandered, tempted by Satan and eventually murdered by His own creation. Through all of this only one thing kept Him from walking away: he was here for a purpose.

We will discuss the relationship between creation and leadership in greater depth in a few chapters, but a fundamental, soul-level understanding that we were created for a purpose is absolutely necessary for us to ever truly lead. One of the harsh realities of life is that situations and people can sometimes be difficult. Things do not always work out the way we hope or plan and sometimes, even though we've put forth our best effort, we have very little to show for it. Unless there is something inside of us that understands we were created to accomplish something important, the desire to quit will be almost impossible to resist when those times come.

In July of 2016 the Veterans Administration published the results of a multi-year study on the mental health of United States Military Veterans. This study dealt specifically with suicides among men and women who have served. Some of their findings were these:

An average of 20 veterans died from suicide every day in 2014.

From 2001 to 2014, the VA found that suicides among U.S. adult civilians increased 23 percent while veteran suicides increased 32 percent, making the risk of suicide 21 percent greater for veterans than civilians (after controlling for age and gender).

In 2014, 7,403 of the 41,425 suicides among U.S. adults that year were committed by veterans.[3]

In our work with the military, statistics like these motivate us to do more and do better to help turn the tide on what has become an epidemic. We have been blessed over the last few years to see, as one measure of program success, a suicide rate of zero among those who have graduated from our programs. While we do not have a perfect program and some people are more impacted than others by what we teach, taking those who are at high risk for suicide and helping them make a positive life decision is something of which we are very proud.

The question, though, is, "Why?" *Why do so many who have attempted suicide, or declared that they will, decide that taking their life is not the answer?* There are a lot of things we say and do during the Mighty Oaks Warrior Programs that work together to bring healing and hope to our students. A key element, however, is that we communicate that we were all created for a purpose, that we all have things to accomplish, and we all have people who need us to get up and lead. So often the hopelessness and despair that ends in taking one's life comes from a sense that there is nothing left to accomplish, that the best days of his life are behind him and the goal now is to simply hang on. When an individual moves from identifying himself with what he has done or what he used to be to understanding that he is created for a purpose still unfulfilled, hope, along with the motivation to get up and lead, returns once more.

2. We must live with the end in mind.

Throughout most of Jesus' ministry, His disciples did not understand that He would eventually be crucified and then ascend back to heaven following His resurrection. When He explained this to them in the 13th chapter of John, they didn't take it very well. They had given up everything to follow Him, and now He was saying He was going to leave. And then He explained why this was all necessary. They were only worried about what they could see and understand, but Jesus had the ability to look at things with the end in mind. In John 14 He said, *"Let not your heart be troubled...I go to prepare a place for you. And if I go and prepare a place for you, I will come again, and receive you unto myself; that where I am, there ye may be also."* To Jesus the crucifixion and resurrection were not the end. They were simply the beginning of an eternal plan. A plan He could walk in with all of the ups and downs because He had the ability to make decisions based on what would be instead of what was.

One of the most difficult parts of leading, whether at home, in the workplace, or in the community, is that it can be hard to know if you are actually making progress. Parents may not really know for years whether their work and sacrifice are adequately preparing their children for life. Doing the right thing at work does not necessarily mean that your boss will notice or that you will get the promotion you were after. Leading in the community may take years before a measurable impact is made. As humans, this lack of immediate impact can cause a lack of motivation to invest our lives in something that requires long-term effort. It used to be that those trying to lose weight and get healthy would measure their progress during a monthly weigh-in session and their annual physical. Today, people wear monitors around their wrist that tell them how they are doing at this exact moment! It has become a fad to wear these devices, and I am convinced that most wearers never actually use them. Getting healthy takes time, but we live in a society that demands instant feedback. Leadership, unfortunately, has a long and often unclear feedback loop.

This is again why our definition of leadership is so important. We use feedback for one of two reasons: to evaluate our progress and make the necessary adjustments for success, or because it makes us feel better about what we're doing. Evaluation is absolutely necessary, particularly over the long-term. We'll talk later about having the right people in your life and just how important that can be. This type of feedback is used to adjust technique but should not impact the leadership principle. When we allow feedback to impact our emotions, we are in a dangerous place. When it feels good and the feedback is positive, we are motivated to continue. When the feedback is lacking or is not what we want it to be, we can lose our motivation and may even decide that it's just not worth it.

When we understand that leadership is *taking people from where they are to where they need to be,* the feedback loop loses its power. We all want to feel good about what we're doing, and it's definitely easier to lead others when you can see progress. If, however, we lead so that we can get others to where they need to be, how we feel about it becomes far less important. We stop worrying about our feelings or the feelings of others and instead focus on the end. We begin to make decisions that will get us to where we're going whether we are happy with where we are or not.

Think of it like a road trip. With very few exceptions, we don't get in our cars because we like to drive. We get in our cars because we have somewhere to go. We sit in traffic, deal with other drivers, and do our best to avoid getting a ticket, not because of how these things make us feel, but because we hope to arrive at our destination. And so it is with our leadership. We need to lead like Jesus did, with the end in mind. It may not make the journey easier, but it will keep us on track when it becomes difficult.

3. It is not about you.

As the moment of the crucifixion drew near, Jesus was arrested in the Garden of Gethsemane after spending most of the night in prayer. When the soldiers approached Him, one of the disciples, Peter, decided that he would fight if necessary to keep Jesus safe. He actually pulled out a sword and cut off the ear of one of the servants that accompanied the guys giving the orders. Jesus' response speaks to the heart of the realization that the things happening were not about Him. After telling Peter to put away his sword and replacing the ear of the servant (an amazing part of the story we often overlook), He said this in Matthew 25:53-54: *"Thinkest thou that I cannot now pray to my Father, and he shall presently give me more than twelve legions of angels? But how then shall the scriptures be fulfilled, that thus it must be?"* What he was saying was profoundly simple. He declared that He was not staying because He could not get away. He was staying because He had a job to do. If getting away or staying safe was the goal, He could have had

10,000 angels come from heaven. But He didn't because it was not about Him.

To me, this is the one of the most difficult things to understand about the life of Jesus. Nothing that He did was done for His own personal benefit. He created the earth and everything on it, and could have done it all again if He wanted to. But He didn't. Instead He did what only He could do—He allowed Himself to be crucified, murdered by His own creation, so that we, humanity, could have our sins forgiven. When we choose to lead, we choose to make life about others instead of ourselves.

There is an interesting verse in Proverbs that speaks about this. Proverbs 13:10 says, "*Only by pride comes contention and with the well advised is wisdom.*" Contention or strife in our relationships only exists when pride is present. Things become difficult in our relationships when we decide that those relationships are about us more than they are about others. And so it is in our leadership. If we do the things we do so that others will benefit, it doesn't really matter what else happens along the way. *Because it isn't about us.*

Unfortunately, leading without concern for our own feelings is not something that comes naturally to us. Jesus is the perfect illustration that we'll never be able to completely emulate. The application, though, is simple. When in the course of your own leadership journey you feel like quitting or become angry and disillusioned because people are not doing what you want them to do, you need to stop and ask yourself, "Why?" *Why did you decide to lead in the first place, and why are you letting how you feel keep you from doing what is right?* Leadership is *taking people from where they are to where they need to be.* Sometimes it's great and other times it's not.

Maybe you've seen the bumper sticker that says, *"I don't know where I'm going, but I'm sure making good time!"* When it comes to leadership, this is where most people live. We have replaced a philosophy of leadership with a collection of techniques and so, although we feel like we're leading, we are actually moving toward an unclear target. Before we can lead in a significant way, we need to define what we're trying to accomplish. Otherwise, even with our best effort given over a lifetime, we can become like the bombers during Operation Cobra. We do everything we're supposed to do, but we hit the wrong target.

Leadership is not a "how" but a "what." It is a lifelong pursuit to make those around you more successful than they would be without you. It is investing your life in helping others *go from where they are to where they need to be.*

Will you decide to lead? The journey begins today.

Discussion Questions

1. What makes defining leadership so difficult? How has a false definition impacted your ability to effectively lead?

2. How does the definition, "Leadership is taking people from where they are to where they need to be," change the way you look at your own leadership? How will this affect your leadership at home? Outside of the home?

3. With this definition in mind, is it possible for everyone to lead? Why or why not?

4. Why is it important to view leadership from the perspective of principle instead of technique? What are some examples?

5. *Give some examples of people in your life who have gotten this right. How did others respond to them?*

Chapter 2
The Need for Leadership

*"The most dangerous leadership myth is that leaders are born-
that there is a genetic factor to leadership. That's nonsense;
in fact, the opposite is true. Leaders are made rather than
born."* [4]

- Warren Bennis

*"Leaders aren't born, they are made. And they are made just
like anything else, through hard work. And that's the price
we'll have to pay to achieve that goal, or any goal."* [5]

- Vince Lombardi

As any parent of small children will tell you, there comes a point
in your life when you realize you know more about cartoon characters
and video games than you do anything of actual significance. Ask me
the plot of the last three Batman cartoon episodes, and I can give you
a complete rundown. Ask me about the current economic situation in
the United States, and I'll have to get back to you.

My wife and I went on a date a few weeks ago to watch a movie
and get something to eat. As we were waiting for the movie to begin, it
occurred to me that the last time I attended a movie *not* produced by

Disney was over ten years ago! I guess at some point you just kind of accept that you'll never again do the things you did before kids. Things like shower without people walking in on you, or getting out of the house without three hours of planning! And while I like books about dogs and dragons and other things that can be described in sentences of six words or less, I get excited when the subject matter is a bit deeper.

Recently, my second-grade son brought home a book about the sinking of the Titanic. It was a simple book written with small children in mind, but at least it was about a real event. While I've never been a student of the Titanic, the movie or the actual event, I enjoyed learning more about it and trying to explain to a seven-year-old how something so tragic could happen. As adults, we learn to accept catastrophe and death as a part of life. We don't like it, but we accept it. My son, however, could not get his mind around the fact that a boat the size of the Titanic could sink and that so many people had died. Talking about this with him caused me to wonder, again, how something of this magnitude could happen. I stayed up one night past my self-imposed 10 p.m. bedtime and did some research to try and understand.

It really is a fascinating story. As you look at the known facts surrounding the sinking of this amazing ship, one thing becomes clear: what caused the sinking of the Titanic was not an iceberg. The Titanic sunk and 1,503 people lost their lives[6] because of a lack of leadership.

Here are some interesting facts about the ship and the events surrounding its sinking:

There were 6 different ice warnings received by the Titanic on the day of the collision.[7]

Despite the ice warnings, the ship was traveling 22.5 knots, just 0.5 knots from its maximum speed.[8]

There were only enough lifeboats for one third of the ship's total capacity.[9]

A lifeboat drill scheduled for earlier the day the ship sank was canceled for an unknown reason.[10]

Two other ships were close enough to rescue survivors but ignored the calls for help.[11]

These stunning circumstances paint a picture of a tragedy that could have been alleviated or avoided altogether if those in charge had demonstrated better leadership. None of this is to suggest that one person was responsible, only that no one person took responsibility for the situation as it unfolded. This is why the story of the Titanic has captured people's imaginations for so long and why my seven-year-old son couldn't understand that it was possible.

As I mentioned in the first chapter, it's amazing how much we can learn from the past. Events like this can teach some incredible truths if we are willing to learn them. One of the major lessons from the sinking of the Titanic is that leadership is the difference between a successful luxury cruise and the type of catastrophe by which all others are judged. This, incidentally, is just as true in every other area of life as it is in the world of cruise lines. A lack of personal leadership will lead to a shipwrecked life. A lack of relational leadership will lead to relational brokenness. A lack of business leadership will lead to failure. Nothing of significance will ever happen without leadership.

If success is based on leadership, why is so much in our world broken? The question we have to ask is, "Where are all of the leaders?" There can only be one answer: the demand for leadership is greater than the supply of those who are able or willing to lead. I am often told by those who opt out of leadership that someone else will lead if they don't. They say this to relieve themselves of the responsibility of leadership. The truth is that although there are many who claim to be leaders and fill positions of leadership, real leaders, people who really understand leadership, are few and far between. And we wonder why our world is falling apart around us.

Since it's so easy to miss things I'm not directly involved in, I wondered if a lack of leadership is an issue dealt in other areas as well. I often tell those who come through our programs that if even a percentage of the nearly 23 million veterans in America began to lead, our communities and our country would be different. Maybe the reason I feel this way is that I live exclusively in the veteran world. *What are people saying about leadership in other places?*

Political Leadership

You don't have to look far to find an opinion on leadership, or the lack thereof, in politics. Having just come through the presidential election of 2016, every show and news article seems to be about our politicians and how they lead or will lead. We even refer to politicians as leaders, calling the President of the United States the leader of the free world.

Knowing that success or failure in any endeavor is largely based on leadership, it is difficult not to conclude that we have some problems. Our world is in absolute chaos, our economy is uncertain, and our liberties continue to erode. I know how all of this makes me feel, *but what about other people?*

The recent "Survey on the Global Agenda" by Shiza Shahid, returned some interesting statistics:

86% of respondents believe there is a global leadership crisis.

Only 55% of respondents have confidence in leaders of non-profit and charitable organizations to advocate for the marginalized and under-represented.

56% of respondents do not have confidence in religious leaders to address global problems.

58% of respondents do not have confidence in government leaders to not abuse their position of authority and power.[12]

All of these are astounding, but the first one taken by itself is incredible: 86% of respondents from countries around the globe feel that there is a global leadership crisis. Clearly, we need qualified, passionate, clear minded leaders to guide the political process and work to bring order and stability to our world.

Business Leadership

In the last ten years Americans have become accustomed to seeing businesses fail that were once cornerstones of the American economy. We have seen government bailouts and other economic controls instituted in an effort to keep these companies around. Unemployment has risen to levels not seen in half a century, and many who are not unemployed find themselves underemployed instead—working but barely making ends meet.

Every time one of these businesses closes its doors, the experts begin to deconstruct their decline. Many factors contributed to the struggles of these companies, but one factor remains consistent. On some level the leader or leaders either created the environment that led to failure or failed to recognize they were in such an environment. In his article *"Businesses Don't Fail, Leaders Do,"* leadership adviser and author Mike Hyatt asserts that the greatest challenge facing businesses is not the economy, but rather those in leadership positions who are either unwilling or unqualified to lead.[13] As the landscape of business continues to change, we must once again ask the question, "Where are all the leaders?"

Church Leadership

Unfortunately, the outlook is not much better for the church. I am a firm believer that the local church is God's plan for spreading the message of the Bible as well as providing an example of that truth lived out. Increasingly, though, neither of these is happening. As the church in America continues to experience an overall decline in attendance as well as a loss of social and cultural influence, and organizations such as the Pew Research Center declares that the U.S. public is becoming less religious,[14] one must ask why. President and CEO of LifeWay Christian Resources, *Thom Rainer*, who has studied church growth and decline for more than 25 years, says this: "Stated simply, the most common factor in declining churches is an inward focus."[15] He continues by explaining that the church in America has become so focused on maintaining the status quo and protecting what was, that there is little room for reaching out. What started as a vehicle for outreach and evangelism has become an institution designed to keep others out. The problem here is the same as in the other areas we have considered: without leaders who are willing to take churches *from where they are to where they need to be*, the church has lost much of its influence. All for lack of leaders.

Why Aren't There More Leaders?

I have had the privilege over the course of my life to spend time with and be influenced by many leaders, *great* ones as well as good ones. So much of who I am as a person has been developed by these men and women whose lives are aligned with the definition of leadership we've outlined. Though they may not define leadership as *taking people from where they are to where they need to be,* they live lives of sacrificial, servant leadership consumed with leveraging their lives and opportunities for others. As I think about their influence in my life, I am reminded of the words of the Apostle Paul in Second Corinthians 12:15. While speaking to a church he cared for deeply, he declared, *"And I will very gladly spend and be spent for you."* Those who have impacted me deeply live that kind of life.

I'm not suggesting that there aren't good leaders in the world. Good leaders can be found in politics, business, the church, and every other area requiring leadership, people who are expending their lives for the good of others. What I am saying, though, is that there are not *enough* good leaders. There are not enough people willing to stand up and help those around them see the way forward.

If this were a problem without a solution, I probably wouldn't spend much time thinking about it. I would write a book on how to survive the coming apocalypse or on the 100 best vacation spots to visit before the end of the world. If this crisis of leadership didn't have a solution, the 189,433 leadership books for sale on Amazon would be better used as fuel in the fires of those without heat in their homes. But there is a solution. Unfortunately, many who have led give up while others who should lead won't start. As Pogo declared in 1970, *"We have met the enemy, and he is us."* [16]

So if a lack of leadership is not due to a lack of available leaders, *why is there such a problem?*

Leadership is Misunderstood

Leadership, like so many other things in life, is defined by experience, background, environment and the example of others in our lives. We misunderstand leadership because instead of a fundamental principle or philosophy of leadership, we look at various techniques and make our own definitions.

For those who have spent time in the military (at least in the infantry), the leader is either the one with the highest rank or the loudest and most aggressive guy in the room. In the Marine Corps co-workers handle their disagreements by going into a room, closing the door, and yelling at each other. The person who quits yelling first loses the argument. That's how I remember it, at least. When I left the Marine Corps to take a position on staff at my church, I quickly found out that churches work differently. Yelling at your co-workers only gets you thrown out of meetings. Defining leadership by the style I had been exposed to made it difficult to transition into a new environment.

For many, the problem is not that they have learned a particular style of leadership, but that they have adopted the idea that you must be a particular kind of person to lead. It's easy to look at the "type A" personalities around us and conclude that we could never do what they do. Maybe we've seen a bad example of leadership, someone who was manipulative and hurtful, and we decided that if that's leadership, *we don't want to be a part of it.* For others, it may simply be an honest self-evaluation. We consider leaders we know, good or bad, and determine that we could never lead. We buy into the idea that leaders are simply born, that leadership is like being human—either you are or you aren't. When we conclude that we are not, *we don't.*

In addition to an accurate definition of leadership, we must understand that *leaders aren't born. They are developed over time* by intentionally becoming the men and women they were created to be. They work to understand their own gifting and limitations and then use them and their unique opportunities to *take others from where they are to where they need to be.* Whether at home, at work, or in the arena of politics, leaders do what is best for those they lead in a style that reflects who they are.

Leaders Fail

A second reason for a lack of leadership is failure. Those who lead will fail from time to time. The job of *taking people from where they are to where they need to be* is a job that is not always met with appreciation and the accolades we equate with leadership. Leadership is often a lonely road filled with more downs than ups. The leader expends the resources of his life for others and fails to meet with the anticipated success.

Sometimes leadership means loss. Loss of those we are trying to lead or those who don't understand. I have met many men and women who used to lead at high levels and stopped because of failures like these. When things don't work out the way we hoped they would, it can be easier to walk away than to figure out why.

Something we must understand if we want to lead is that failure happens but it does not define who we are. I have failed, but that does not make me a failure. It makes me fallible, it makes me human, and it even makes me a jerk sometimes, but it does not make me a failure. The Bible talks about this in Psalms and Proverbs. Speaking of the person following God, the Psalmist says in Psalm 37:24, *"Though he fall, he shall not be utterly cast down."* Proverbs 24:16 declares, *"For a just man falleth seven times and riseth up again."* When leaders begin to define themselves by either the successes or failures that have taken place in their leadership, they are on dangerous ground. When you're good, you're not that good and when you're bad, you're not that bad. Failure, if seen as a reflection of the person instead of just an event, will cause even the best leader to quit.

Another type of failure that sidelines many is the failure of others. Unless a leader has the ability to dictate the behavior of others, people follow because they have some degree of confidence in the one leading. We must have some measure of faith in those we look to for direction or we would never do what they say. So we follow, and as we follow, our confidence in the leader grows. They have kept their word and followed through on their promises, and, although we know they aren't perfect, they've demonstrated good judgment. Then something happens. Maybe we find out they are not all we believed them to be. They have been intentionally deceptive, and we feel foolish for trusting them. Perhaps they fall morally or steal from the company. Whatever the case, it is possible that someone in whom we have placed trust and confidence will fail.

When this happens, it can cause us to question whether any part of their leadership was real. We're hurt because we feel betrayed, and we begin to look at everything that leader was involved in as fraudulent. We simply want to walk away.

And many do. They quit, not because they have failed, but because of the failure of someone else in their life. While I would never attempt to diminish the pain caused by someone who forgets that leadership is about others, I would challenge anyone who has been let down by a leader to not allow someone else's failure to keep them from moving forward.

Two things are true. First, my responsibility is to do what I know is right. I am not responsible for the actions or failures of others. Secondly, as the familiar adage says, it takes a lifetime to build a good reputation and just one moment to ruin it. Just as we do not want our life to be judged by our mistakes and failures, we should not dismiss the good done by others because of the bad. We need to be intentional about living lives that won't be knocked off course when those we trust fail.

Nothing Worthwhile Comes Without a Fight

As I consider the many reasons there are not more leaders, I firmly believe that this is one of the most significant. Leadership, the kind that puts others first, is extremely difficult. We like to think of a leader as the guy we celebrate for winning the battle or overcoming some overwhelming obstacle. The truth is, leadership is often lonely and thankless. For every minute of positive recognition there are many more minutes of criticism, loneliness, frustration and loss. Leaders stop leading when the trials of leadership become so overwhelming that the victories seem meaningless to them. Many others never begin to lead because the uphill climb of leadership is more than they are willing to endure. Many like the idea of being the leader or the title of leader, but few actually understand and embrace the bad of leadership that comes from the good.

When teaching this to leaders struggling to get back up, I'm often asked, "What makes leadership so difficult? Why is it such a fight to invest in others and to help them get where they need to go?" Here are a few of the many answers.

Leadership is difficult because:

1. We often become our own worst enemy. We are selfish by nature. This is what keeps us alive. We find food to satisfy our hunger, shelter to make us comfortable, and companionship to make us happy. The challenge is that sacrificing our own ambitions and desires so that we can take people from where they are to where they need to be runs contrary to our selfish nature. It doesn't come naturally. At some point in our leadership journey we have to make a decision to lead regardless of the cost to us personally, something that many are simply unwilling to do.

2. Sacrificial leadership runs contrary to our culture. Many people present themselves as warriors for social justice or the champions of the forgotten, but often even these efforts are about self-aggrandizement and notoriety. If you were to ask the average volunteer at a local non-profit why they volunteer, you will most probably get the answer, "Because it makes me feel good." Even service is about us and not others. Our culture is built on the idea of doing what is best for me and those I care about. Real leaders must swim against this stream, a burden that many aren't willing to bear.

3. The willingness of young adults to embrace the mantle of leadership in homes and business and in other areas of life continues to diminish. A mountain of research has been done on the length of time young people are now taking to move out of their parents' homes, secure full-time employment, and step into leadership roles, but we have yet to understand the long-term impact of these trends. The more we teach young people they need to make decisions based only on their personal welfare, the less people we'll see willing to lead.

4. Institutions that once taught leadership are growing silent. Churches and civic organizations once taught leadership as a fundamental principle. Leading in the home and leading in the community were expected of the members of these organizations. But the focus has shifted inward. These organizations want to protect themselves more than they want to leverage their influence and opportunity for the benefit of others.

Regardless of where you want to lead, it's going to be difficult. But nothing worthwhile comes without a fight. You will have to fight human nature, established cultural norms, and the opinions of others. It will not be easy, but living a life of purpose and serving others is always worth it. As I think of this principle, I am reminded of a speech by *Theodore Roosevelt* called "The Man in the Arena":

> *It is not the critic who counts; not the man who points out how the strong man stumbles, or where the doer of deeds could have done them better. The credit belongs to the man who is actually in the arena, whose face is marred by dust and sweat and blood; who strives valiantly; who errs, who comes short again and again, because there is no effort without error and shortcoming; but who does actually strive to do the deeds; who knows great enthusiasms, the great devotions; who spends himself in a worthy cause; who at the best knows in the end the triumph of high achievement, and who at the worst, if he fails, at least fails while daring greatly, so that his place shall never be with those cold and timid souls who neither know victory nor defeat.*[17]

The need for leaders is great. For the one willing to lead, the opportunities are everywhere. Before anyone can begin to lead or stand back up and begin leading again, they have to decide. Leadership is a process that takes place over a lifetime, a process that begins with the first step of decision.

What about you? Will you decide today to step into the role you have been created to fulfill and begin *taking people from where they are to where they need to be?*

Discussion Questions

1. Why is there such a need for leaders in our world? What keeps people from leading?

2. Do you agree or disagree with the premise that leadership is the thing that makes the difference between success and failure? Why?

3. How has leadership failure, either personal or from others, impacted how you lead and how you think about leadership?

4. Is there a need for leadership in your relationships? Which ones? What can you do about it?

Chapter 3

The Leader and Creation

"There are no ordinary people. You have never met a mere mortal." [18]

- C.S. Lewis

"Our worth is connected to our Creator. If God is of great and inestimable worth, then human beings made in his image must be of great value, too." [19]

- Art Lindsley

Why do leaders lead? This is a question I've been asked, heard discussed, and from time to time even offered my own opinion on. It's a great question because if we had the answer, we would understand why some leaders stop leading and why others never begin.

In William Shakespeare's comedy *The Twelfth Night,* his main character Malvolio declares, "Some are born great, some achieve greatness, and some have greatness thrust upon 'em."[20] This statement describes how most people view leadership. Some, because of station in life or education or some unusual opportunity, are destined to be leaders. Others lead, perhaps reluctantly, because they have to and there is no one more qualified around. The third category involves those who become leaders because of sheer will and their ability to get what they want.

While many people do find themselves in positions of leadership for one of these reasons, none of these make a person a leader. As we've discussed previously, there are two problems with defining leadership by a position or personality or unusual opportunity. First, when things become difficult, those who are leading simply quit. Since it's not as much about the leader as it is about a position, they have no reason to continue in the face of opposition. Secondly, people without any of the things described conclude they should never even begin.

Having spent much of my adult life around those who have served or are serving in the military, I have seen how the wrong answer to the question of why leaders lead can impact careers, families, and, in many cases, lives. This isn't only true for those who have served, but there are few places like the military that take the topic of leadership so seriously and where those who have led decide that it is no longer important.

One story in particular sticks out to me. I met Dan on his first day as a student at one of our Mighty Oaks Programs. I didn't know much about him at the time except that he was a retired Marine Sergeant Major. As the session began, Dan seemed just like the other men in attendance. He had served proudly and honorably in the Marine Corps but now looked like someone without hope who was carrying the weight of nearly thirty years of service and a lot of brokenness on his shoulders. It was clear that he didn't want to be there, but also that he had nowhere else to go.

As the week unfolded and he became more comfortable with our team and the process we were taking him through, Dan shared the details of his life's story and what brought him to his current station in life. He was raised by his mom and abusive father in a small Midwestern town with little to do but get in trouble. Growing up, he said, he would get into trouble with friends, but the trouble with his dad was worse. His father was an alcoholic who would become violent when drinking. Dan decided at a young age that as soon as he could leave home, he would and that he didn't really care where he went.

His opportunity came just as he was turning 18 when a Marine Corps recruiter convinced him that he could have a future serving in the Marines. Dan was looking for a way out, and since the recruiter could get him into basic training the next week, he signed up and shipped off. For the next thirty years, Dan served with honor and distinction, achieving the highest enlisted rank possible, the rank of Sergeant Major. He served in both peacetime and war, leading thousands of Marines in locations around the world. Dan is a humble guy and shared this story as just a series of facts. The rest of the story, though, he told with a great deal of emotion.

Throughout his years of service, the one thing that he was never able to figure out was the relationships in his life. While he was leading Marines around the globe, he was never able to lead his family. He has been married several times and hasn't spoken to his children in years. Then he explained what brought him to our program. Even though he had a career that spanned three decades and was successful from nearly every perspective, it didn't end that way. Broken relationships and a change in job responsibilities caused him to lose his way and abuse alcohol to the point where retirement became a mandatory event. He left the only thing he had ever really known and was now without purpose or direction.

It wasn't long before life had so little purpose to Dan that the only thing that made sense was taking his own life. It was a suicide attempt that led him to us. A failed attempt caused his family to reach out to Mighty Oaks, and his first stop after recovering was one of our programs. Dan is doing great now and is working to rebuild his life and move forward in a meaningful way.

Whenever I hear stories like this, I wonder how someone can look like they have it all figured out but be so lost and broken. I asked Dan how he went from a place of remarkable success to utter desperation, and he said what I have heard many others say. He said that when his purpose, leading Marines, was taken away, he didn't feel like he had anything to live for. He knew how to lead Marines but didn't know how to lead a home or family, so he saw no point in continuing. It wasn't until he found his purpose in Christ that things began to make sense. When he realized he was created with purpose and a design, the rest of his life came in to focus.

Dan's story is not uncommon. I could share many more just like it. This scenario isn't unique to the military, but it always amazes me how an institution that puts so much emphasis on leadership misses its essence. Equating leadership with a job or personality type sets leaders up for failure when the job is taken away or they no longer "feel" like a leader. And so, with nearly 23 million veterans in America, trained leaders are in every community in our country but no longer leading because they have left the jobs that defined them. This is what makes the last part of Dan's story so important. When he realized he was *created* with purpose and design, the rest of his life came into focus.

Why do leaders lead? They lead because they were created to lead! When this truth is embraced, the job title, the personality and the opportunities become far less important. Leading, *taking others from where they are to where they need to be*, is what all of us were created to do. Until we understand this, we will always struggle with leadership.

In the Beginning

The story in Genesis 1 is incredible. God, who is without beginning, created the earth and all its inhabitants. He started by speaking the earth itself into existence. He then separated the light from the darkness and set boundaries for the oceans. And as if speaking the world into existence wasn't enough, He filled it with unimaginable beauty. The thousands of plants, flowers, and trees that provide both color and texture to the planet were seen for the first time. I can't imagine what this all must have looked like in its perfect state. Then it was time for the animals—animals of every kind spoken into existence to enjoy the perfect environment that had been created.

Today, when we talk about someone who is creative, we are talking about someone who can take what has already been done and build on it or adjust it or interpret it in a new way. When God created, He made something out of nothing! The unfathomable creativity of God can be seen in all of nature. Simply considering the variety of plants and animals should cause us to stand in awe of who He is and what He can do!

After all of this, He had one more thing to create. Genesis 1:26-27 and 2:7 says:

And God said, Let us make man in our image, after our likeness: and let them have dominion over the fish of the sea, and over the fowl of the air, and over the cattle, and over all the earth, and over every creeping thing that creepeth upon the earth. So God created man in his own image, in the image of God created he him; male and female created he them.

And the LORD God formed man of the dust of the ground, and breathed into his nostrils the breath of life; and man became a living soul.

Do not miss what these verses are saying. Read them again if you need to and let the truth of the words sink in. God created everything by speaking. Incredible! Our planet is a system so complex that we still don't understand how it all works, and yet it came into existence because God spoke.

With man, however, things were different. God did not simply speak man into existence as he had the animals, thousands of which were spoken into existence at one time, all complex and beautiful. When it came to man, God became very specific and very intentional. Man was created in the image of the Creator with the breath of life breathed into him by God! Mankind is not simply another animal existing to live in harmony with the other animals, but rather the image bearer of the one who made it all!

That singular truth should be enough to help us understand that each of us was created for a specific purpose with a specific calling that transcends a job or relationships or type of personality. When we consider the level of care taken by an eternal God to bring mankind into existence, we cannot help but conclude that as long as we are drawing breath He has something for us to do.

So what exactly does it mean to be created in the image of God? We could talk about a number of things here, but since we can't cover everything, let's look at three very important ones.

Created with Purpose

Does my life really have purpose? This is a question all of us will deal with from time to time and a question that, depending on our answer, will either encourage us to move forward or cause us to quit. If we believe that we have purpose, then we must also conclude that we have value. Understanding that we have value motivates us to move forward in a meaningful way as we attempt to fulfill our purpose in our day-to-day lives. If, on the other hand, we conclude that we do not have a purpose other than survival, the logical decision is to simply quit since a life without purpose is a life without value. People quit jobs, families, and sometimes even their lives when they conclude that it doesn't matter anyway.

A clear understanding of purpose and the value that flows from that purpose is so important. When we find our purpose in a job or a relationship, we will lose that purpose if the circumstances of either change. But if we accept that we were created with purpose, the circumstances of life have no impact on whether we consider ourselves valuable. God's specific will for every person isn't the same, and living in His will doesn't mean that we will have an easy life. But every person, regardless of vocation, station in life, or background, has a unique purpose given by the Creator. Embracing that purpose brings the fulfillment to life that so many are missing. As Dick Staub has said, "You will feel the greatest pleasure and wholeness when who God made you to be is fully developed and expressed."[21]

There have been times when I've felt lost or overwhelmed by the circumstances around me. But since I know that God created me for a purpose, I am able to continue moving forward without losing hope. I may lose my way from time to time, but I will never lose the purpose that was given to me at creation.

Given a Plan

When we understand that we were created with purpose, the natural question to ask is, "How do I find that purpose?" How often we say something like, "If life came with an instruction manual, this would be so much easier." I've said that many times. Whether it is relationships or raising children or planning for the future, this whole thing would be so much easier if only we had a plan to follow.

The truth is, we do have a plan. It was given to us by our Creator, so that regardless of the situations we find ourselves in, we will know how to function according to our design. This plan doesn't deal with specific cultural or societal situations or the thousands of other things we'll encounter over the course of a lifetime, but it does teach us how to live within the framework of design. So many people live outside of their intended purpose and wonder why they lack the fulfillment and direction they want so badly. They fill their days with things that should bring that fulfillment but consistently come up empty without understanding why. Since God created us, He fully understands our capacity and the weaknesses that will undermine the purpose He has for us.

Because He understands both our human weakness and our incredible potential, He worked through human authors to provide us with the Bible. The Bible is the plan or the instruction manual of life. It doesn't address all of the decisions you'll need to make, but when you begin to follow its guidelines, the decisions that are specific to you are no longer overwhelming and unknowable. God wants us to succeed in everything He's given to us to do, and he gave us the instructions necessary for that success.

The Bible though is not just an abstract list of do's and don'ts. I like to reference the instructions when I am attempting a difficult project. I know that men generally have a bad reputation when it comes to instructions, but I am not one of *those* men. I always start with the instructions because I've had too many projects that ended with me holding extra parts. I have found, however, I do better when I watch the directions than when I read them. The ancient proverb, "YouTube is your friend," definitely rings true in my life. When I can watch a video where the instructor not only tells me how to do something but shows me how to as well, I will have no problem accomplishing the task at hand. Observing the finished product sometimes makes getting to the finished product possible.

God, because He created us, knows that simply telling us what to do, while it should be enough, just isn't. He has had men and women for thousands of years proclaim His message to us, which, again, should be enough. But sometimes that message falls on deaf ears or unwilling hearts. So He gave us a picture of how the purpose He has built into us is supposed to work.

Earlier we said that the life of Jesus illustrates the definition of leadership, *taking people from where they are to where they need to be.* When we look at the Bible as a whole, though, we see that the life of Christ on this earth is just a part of that illustration. The entire story of the Bible is an example of God the Creator taking His creation from *where they were to where they needed to be.*

Following the creation of man, Adam and Eve exercised their free will against God and did exactly what He told them not to do. We could use a lot of different words to describe their action, but the word "sin" is the most specific. It was a rebellion against the authority of God that brought judgment. This is how the story of the Bible begins.

The New Testament begins with Christ giving His life to pay the price for that sin and make forgiveness and a relationship with God once again possible. He took mankind from where they were under the judgment of sin to where they needed to be, a place of forgiveness and relationship. The Bible ends with the ultimate victory for man by God. Around those two events is the rest of the Bible. While some may look at the Bible as a series of disjointed stories, the entirety of the Bible is God exercising His divine sovereignty (supreme power or authority)[22] over history to make this forgiveness and restoration possible.

From the moment man sinned, God put in motion the plan to *take him from where he is to where he needs to be.* The first thing that God did after Adam and Eve sinned was to tell them that the one who would provide forgiveness would come. He gave them hope. And then, as we work through the Old Testament we see promises and pictures that all pointed to the coming hope. God worked through men and events to create the needed circumstances for Jesus to come to this earth, and at the time that had been prophesied thousands of years earlier, He did. All of this was done because mankind needed divine leadership that would take him from where he was in brokenness and sin to where he needed to be in a relationship with the Creator. The Bible is not a collection of unrelated historical anecdotes, but an amazing picture of leadership from the Creator on the behalf of His creation.

Now let me make this clear: the ultimate purpose of man is the worship of God. Revelation 4:11 puts it this way: "Thou art worthy, O Lord, to receive glory and honor and power: for thou hast created all things, and for thy pleasure they are and were created." We were created to worship God by honoring Him in all we do. To worship God simply means that our goal is to bring Him glory in every aspect of our lives. We do this by living, not for ourselves, but for Him. The real question for most of us is, *how do we do that?* By following the instruction manual and living according to His example. We glorify God most when we fulfill the purpose He created in each one of us. We glorify Him when we dedicate ourselves to *leading* others from *where they are to where they need to be.* This is the ultimate expression of God's purpose through us. We were given different gifts and opportunities but all were given so that we can fulfill our big purpose of bringing honor to God by serving others. We honor Him most when we use those specific talents and opportunities to lead others from where they are to where they need to be just as He modeled for us in the Bible.

You and I can decide how we will live. It is only when we align those decisions with what the Bible, God's plan for life, says that we will fulfill the purpose for which we were created. *How can I know God's purpose for me.* Live to worship Him by aligning your gifts, talents and opportunities to the example that He has already provided.

Existing Eternally

Perhaps what impacts me most when I consider that I was created in the God's image is the truth that what I do in my lifetime will have eternal implications. It is so easy to get caught up in the mundane of life that we forget there's something bigger. The things that we do during our years on this earth will have an impact on our eternal life and that of those we have the opportunity to influence. We will spend an entire chapter on how to leave a legacy, but as we consider our creation, it is essential that we realize we were not just created to fill up the space between birth and death, but that we were created to impact eternity!

Do the things you're investing your life in reflect an understanding of the eternal nature of your creation? Someday, how you lived will be revealed. The Bible puts it this way in First Corinthians 3:13: *"Every man's work shall be made manifest: for the day shall declare it, because it shall be revealed by fire; and the fire shall try every man's work of what sort it is."* If the substance of your life were placed in a pile and fire was used to burn off all the stuff that just didn't matter, *what would be left?* For those who understand that they were created with an eternal purpose, life is about leaving the stuff that the fire cannot burn.

Real leaders lead because leadership, living to *take people from where they are to where they need to be,* was created within us. When we were made in the image of God, we were made to glorify Him by leading others. Life will have its extreme highs and lows and a lot of time somewhere in the middle. There will be things that we enjoy doing and things that we would rather avoid. But nothing will keep a leader from leading when they grasp the truth that they have a purpose bigger than anything that will happen in their life. We were created with a purpose and a plan that allow us to make an eternal impact with the moments we have been given. Live the life that you were created to live. Live the life of a leader.

Discussion Questions

1. Why is it significant, as it relates to our topic of leadership, that God did not create man the way He created everything else?

2. How does knowing that we were created with purpose change your outlook on life and your place of leadership?

3. What does the following quote by Dick Staub mean: "You will feel the greatest pleasure and wholeness when who God made you to be is fully developed and expressed."

4. Does understanding that we all have an eternal existence change your perspective on what you do right now? In what way?

5. Why do leaders lead?

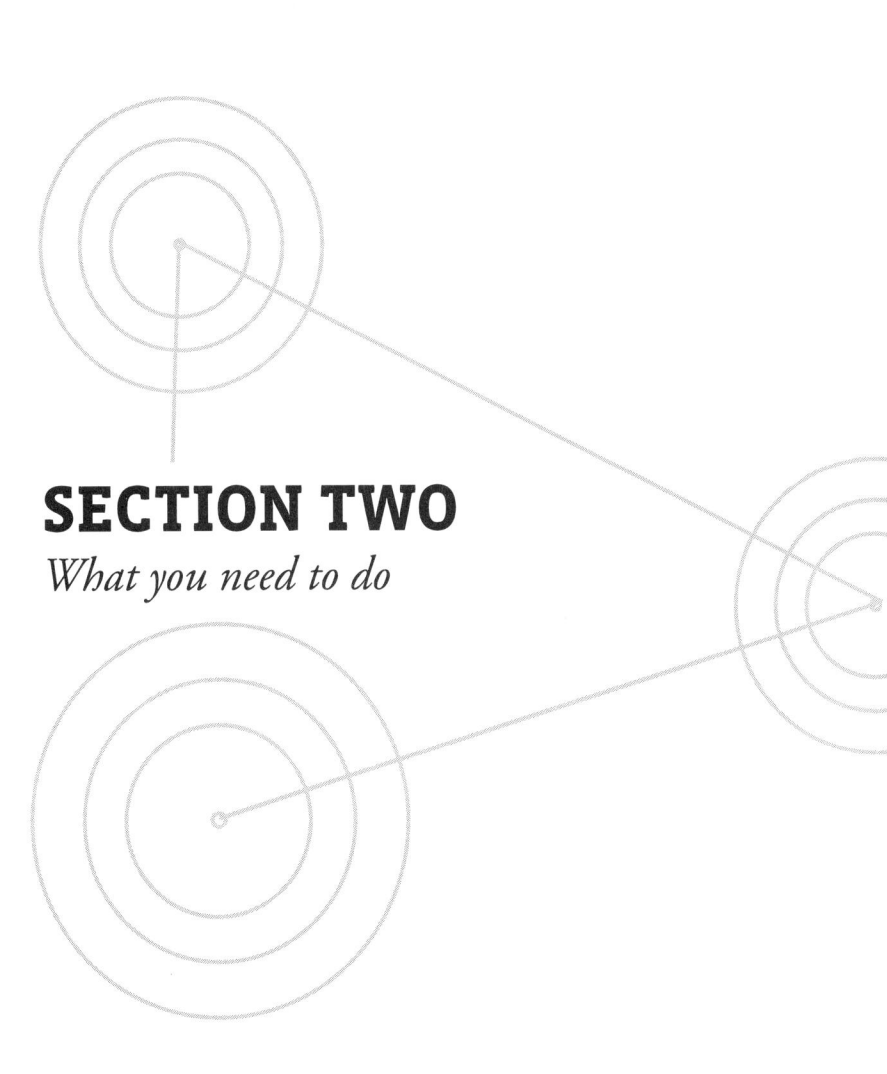

SECTION TWO

What you need to do

Chapter 4

Believe the Truth

"Beliefs are the rails upon which our lives run. We almost always act according to what we really believe." [23]

- J.P. Moreland

Life has a way of not only humbling us but also teaching lessons that impact the way we view the world. For me, one of those lessons came when the war in Iraq began. From the time I was fourteen years old until the First Marine Division deployed to Kuwait, shortly after my 26th birthday, my life was pointed toward leading Marines in combat. It sounds like an odd life goal, but for me, I could imagine no greater test than leading men against the enemy. I worked hard to achieve this goal, attending schools that would prepare and train me so I would know what to do when the time came. When we were told we'd be deploying, I wasn't interested in the reason. I was finally going to do what I had dreamed about for more than ten years.

Some of the people in my life did care about the reason, however. About a week before I left for what would become a historic deployment, my mom pulled me aside at a family gathering and asked if I felt comfortable supporting this operation. She didn't offer her own political commentary but wanted to know that I was okay with it. I'm pretty sure I didn't give her the answer she was looking for, responding as only someone too naive to know better could. I proudly told her that those in the military do not have the luxury of asking why, that we went where the Commander in Chief told us to go, and that I would do my job regardless of the reason. I didn't need to believe it was right; I just needed to do what I had been trained to do.

The war in Iraq began a few months later as the Fifth Marines (my unit) breached the berm between Kuwait and Iraq and started a road march that would end in Baghdad. For the first time in my life, I was watching tracers come back my direction. Unlike in training, losing here meant people would die. The moment was surreal.

It's funny what you think about at times like that. With as much clarity as if I had been sitting in my parent's house, right there in the middle of the night with chaos all around, I remembered my mom asking me if I believed we were doing the right thing by going to Iraq. When I was safe at home I could give platitudes about how unimportant belief was. When the enemy was real, what I believed became very important. I did believe we were doing the right thing, and through many long and confusing days that belief kept me going.

What do you believe? The answer to this question will profoundly influence the decisions you make and the course you set for your life, whether you want it to or not. What you believe will not only set you on the right path, but will keep you there when things get tough. Belief can keep someone pushing through a bad situation to a hoped-for end or cause them to quit when things get overwhelming. Belief can turn a bad marriage into a good one or cause two people who once loved each other to walk away. Belief is often the difference between winning and losing in nearly every area of life. Belief, whether positive or negative, will impact you.

As a leader, you must have the right beliefs or you will not be able to effectively *take people from where they are to where they need to be.* If you don't believe that you can, then you can't. And this is where many leaders begin to drift. They stop believing that it's possible, and they quit. They stop believing that *they* can lead. They start to listen to the voices in their head that say things like, "You can't do this," or, "You are no longer qualified to help others," and they stop doing what they were created to do. A leader must believe the truth about himself and his qualifications to lead or it's just a matter of time before he won't lead at all.

I love the Bible for many reasons, but a big one is the colorful cast of characters we find on almost every page. Throughout its sixty-six books we find those who were great and those who were not so great, people of great faith, people trying to find a reason to believe, and people who did their best but had real life struggles. One of those people was a man named Paul.

Paul was a man who influenced Christianity more profoundly than probably any other person in History. He started churches throughout the world and wrote most of the New Testament at the same time. What we know about Christianity and God's plan for man in the modern age was either influenced by or came directly from Paul. He is an example of leadership that anyone would do well to emulate.

Thankfully he was not afraid to share his weaknesses as well as his strengths. He talks openly about the seasons in his life when he struggled with doubt. The most important part of his vulnerability is that he shares where his belief rested when he began to doubt. We need to believe the right thing in order to end up in the right place, *but what do we do when our belief begins to fail?*

A Strong Start

Paul the Apostle was a man who not only had the call of God on his life, but also had the education and experience to spread the gospel message effectively. I often talk to people who feel like their life experiences have been wasted or that what they're doing now has nothing to do with their past. When I have these conversations, I try to remind them that we never know how God will use our past experiences and education to equip us for what He's planned for our lives.

We see this in the life of Paul. As a young man he was educated as a teacher of Jewish law. Much of this law was established by God in the Old Testament of the Bible, but much of the law that governed the lives and behavior of Jews was in addition to the God-given law of the Old Testament. Paul's education in this law was the best possible. In fact, we're told that Paul's mentor was a man by the name of Gamaliel who was well respected in the governing body of Judaism. We could say that Paul's education was of the caliber of a modern-day Ivy League university or law school degree. And then, everything changed.

Paul's job was enforcing the law on the Jews who put their faith in Jesus instead of the Old Testament law. While traveling, he had an encounter with Christ. We're told in Acts 9 that Christ showed Himself to Paul, and at that moment, Paul surrendered to Christ as the Savior. Once converted, Paul put as much passion and energy into the work of spreading the salvation message as he had once put into stopping that same message. Acts 9:22 says, *"But Saul* [Paul's name prior to conversion] *increased the more in strength, and confounded the Jews which dwelt at Damascus, proving that this is very Christ."*

This experience started an amazing work in his life that didn't end until he died. We know both from scripture and secular history that after a period of training, Paul traveled the world starting churches and preaching that Jesus is God. His life ended after a defense of the Gospel in Rome that led to his martyrdom.

One of the intriguing things about his life is how much his pre-conversion experience and education equipped him to do the work he did. The book of Romans is the great apologetic book of scripture; Paul eloquently explains the gospel in a way only one trained to lay out a logical defense of fact could explain it. Paul was able to do this as a trained attorney gifted in logical communication, but also because the area of law he studied was that of the Jewish religious system. Were it not for his education and experience, he wouldn't have understood the argument well enough to lay out the case for faith he so clearly expounds. God used his life experience and education to change the world by bringing the pieces together for one pre-ordained purpose.

This part of Paul's life encourages me when I consider that God's plan is bigger than the moment I find myself in and that He will use the things I've learned and experienced to bring about His plan if I trust Him. It's extremely appropriate, given his story, that Paul penned the words of Romans 8:28: *"And we know that all things work together for good to them that love God, to them who are the called according to his purpose."* Paul was used greatly by God because he trusted God even when the path in front of him was unclear.

A Lingering Past

Here is where the story of Paul's life speaks to me in a very personal way. I am so thankful that the Bible doesn't just share the good of people's lives but the bad as well. Before Paul became a Christian he took the job of ending Christianity very seriously. The Jewish rulers of the day saw the followers of Jesus as blaspheming God and a threat to their way of life and their control. Since they were unwilling to see that Jesus was the fulfillment of the law they so passionately defended, the only alternative was to persecute those who did. And Paul was one of their most passionate enforcers.

Acts 8 tells us just how passionate he was. The first recorded Christian martyr, Steven, dies in chapter 7. He was stoned to death for preaching that Jesus is God, and Saul (later called Paul) was there watching it all happen. The story picks up in chapter 8 verse 1:

> *And Saul was consenting unto his death. And at that time there was a great persecution against the church, which was at Jerusalem; and they were all scattered abroad throughout the regions of Judaea and Samaria, except the apostles. 2 And devout men carried Stephen to his burial, and made great lamentation over him. 3 As for Saul, he made havoc of the church, entering into every house, and haling men and women committed them to prison. 4 Therefore they that were scattered abroad went everywhere preaching the word.*

The story continues in chapter 9:

> *And Saul, yet breathing out threatenings and slaughter against the disciples of the Lord, went unto the high priest, 2 And desired of him letters to Damascus to the synagogues, that if he found any of this way, whether they were men or women, he might bring them bound unto Jerusalem.*

That's pretty strong language. Paul was "breathing out threatenings and slaughter" and going from house to house persecuting those who trusted in Christ! To put it mildly, he was not a good person. Reflecting on his life, Paul describes himself in I Timothy 1:15 as the "chief of sinners." In First Corinthians 15:9 he says, *"For I am the least of the apostles, that am not meet to be called an apostle, because I perse-cuted the church of God."* We aren't sure what exactly those statements include, but it's clear that Paul was a man with a past that he couldn't forget and that, at least some of the time, caused him to feel that he was unqualified for ministry. In Romans 7:20, after a dissertation on sin and its work in a life, he makes this statement: *"O wretched man that I am! Who shall deliver me from the body of this death?"*

This was Paul, who received his life purpose directly from Jesus speaking from heaven; the great Apostle who was used to start churches and accomplish the work for which he had been trained, equipped and sent out; the man to whom modern Christianity owes much of its doctrine. And yet, with a resume that would make most of us jealous, his understanding of his own struggles and inadequacy, together with a history of fighting the truth, caused him to conclude that he was wretched and in need of deliverance.

I don't take comfort in the anguish of others, but I do take com-fort in knowing that others experience anguish. The fact is that no one knows us as well as we know us. We do our best to keep others from seeing the hurt and doubt that all of us carry around. We think about the times in life when we've failed, decisions that we've rethought a thousand times and destructive behaviors that we would immediately change if only we had the power. All these things together can cause the best of us to say something similar to the statement made by Paul: *"I am such a mess, who can help me?"*

It is these thoughts and the feelings that accompany them that cause many educated, equipped, sent-out leaders to decide they are no longer qualified to lead. People will talk about lacking a clear purpose as the reason they don't lead. I believe that lack of clarity isn't the real reason—it's the insecurity of understanding just how inadequate we really are. Believing we aren't qualified causes us to stop doing what we are uniquely qualified to do.

New Ground

Paul may have been clear on his own past and personal shortcomings, but he didn't let that keep him from going forward. We see how he was able to move forward when we read Romans 8:1: *"There is therefore now no condemnation to them which are in Christ Jesus, who walk not after the flesh, but after the Spirit."*

What an amazing transition from inadequacy and insecurity to absolute victory! In chapters 7 and 8 of Romans Paul explains the futility of trying to do it on our own and the absolute power of understanding that victory is only possible through Jesus Christ. Paul accomplished incredible feats not because he had a flawless past or because he had his life together but because his confidence was in the work done by the Savior that he proclaimed! His belief—not in himself or his education or even his calling, but in God—is what gave him the ability to accomplish the purpose he was born for.

Why does he say this? Some of his other statements help to provide insight:

> *"Nay, in all these things we are more than conquerors through him that loved us. 38 For I am persuaded, that neither death, nor life, nor angels, nor principalities, nor powers, nor things present, nor things to come, 39 Nor height, nor depth, nor any other creature, shall be able to separate us from the love of God, which is in Christ Jesus our Lord" (Romans 8:37-38).*

> *"But thanks be to God, which giveth us the victory through our Lord Jesus Christ" (First Corinthians 15:57).*

"Now thanks be unto God, which always causeth us to triumph in Christ, and maketh manifest the savior of his knowledge by us in every place" (Second Corinthians 2:14).

"Therefore if any man be in Christ, he is a new creature: old things are passed away; behold, all things are become new" (Second Corinthians 5:17).

What Paul believed and what every leader needs to believe is that when we have an authentic relationship with God through Christ, our identity is found in Him, not in who we were, what we think, or even how we feel. When man rebelled against God, the fellowship between the created and the Creator was broken. This broken fellowship made it impossible for mankind to fulfill the purpose he was created for. It was only the intervention of God through His Son Jesus Christ that forgiveness of sin and restoration of that relationship was possible.

From the moment man first sinned he was under the penalty of that sin and spiritually dead. Christ's perfect life, death on the cross, and victorious resurrection paid for sin so that man wouldn't have to. When man is willing to acknowledge his sin, ask forgiveness of a Holy God, and put his faith in what Jesus did for him, he is made alive and his relationship with God is restored!

This restored relationship is what makes victory possible. It's what makes fulfilling a life purpose possible. It is this belief, the belief that we are victorious because of what Christ has done, that gives us the strength and the courage to lead and continue leading even when we feel inadequate or unqualified. For those of us who have accepted His gift of forgiveness, we are not striving for victory but living in the victory He has already secured.

What do you believe? The answer to this question will have a profound impact on the decisions you make and the direction in which you live. The answer to this question will largely determine whether you will fulfill the purpose for which you were created. Your past does not dictate your future and your shortcomings do not determine whether you are qualified. When you believe that it is about what Jesus has done instead of what you've failed to do, you are ready to lead!

Discussion Questions

1. How does belief impact the things you do? What are some examples (both good and bad) of decisions you've made based on belief?

2. What are some things that cause us to believe the wrong things about our ability to lead others?

3. How did the Apostle Paul get beyond his negative beliefs, and what does that mean for you?

4. What is the importance to belief to an authentic relationship with God?

5. Are you pursuing victory in your life by living in the victory provided by Christ?

Chapter 5

Be a Person of Character

I have a dream that my four little children will one day live in a nation where they will not be judged by the color of their skin but by the content of their character.[24]

-Martin Luther King Jr.

Character is like a tree and reputation like a shadow. The shadow is what we think of it; the tree is the real thing.[25]

-Abraham Lincoln

Several years ago when my family and I were living in Oceanside California, we took an afternoon and went to the beach. This was something we always enjoyed, particularly since the house we lived in was only a few miles away. We only had two kids at the time, but it was still a bit of a chore getting packed and then unpacked and set up at our favorite spot. Once we were there, though, the kids could play while we relaxed.

On this particular day, I must have relaxed a little too much because as I lay on my towel I began to fall asleep. Most of the time I did my best to pay attention to what the kids were doing for fear of drowning or strangers or sharks. I always joke that I can't let anything bad happen to the kids because of how angry their mom would be with me. But truthfully, as fun as days at the beach can be, a lot of things can go wrong if you're not careful. On this day, though, I was completely oblivious.

What pulled me out of my slumber was the laughter of the people sitting around us. They began laughing pretty hard, so I had to sit up to see what was going on. If you've ever fallen asleep in the sun you know that it takes a minute for your eyes to adjust when you first open them. At first you can only see outlines until the full picture becomes clear. When I opened my eyes, I could see the outline of a boy, about four years old, standing at the edge of the surf. As the picture became clear I noticed he had his shorts around his ankles and his hands on his hips. Apparently that's what you do when you relieve yourself in the ocean! The last thing to become clear was the identity of this child; it was my *wife's* son!

Truthfully it was my son as well, but at times like those you keep as much distance as possible. I heard one of the laughing ladies ask, "I wonder who this kid belongs to?" I just looked around as though I wasn't sure either. I think everyone figured it out, though, when he ran over to me and asked for help pulling his shorts up. I believe in correcting my kids in private whenever possible, but this was definitely the time to let him know, for the benefit of our audience, that public urination is not okay.

With my best tone of surprise, I asked him why in the world he would go to the bathroom on the beach. His answer did not improve my reputation with the bystanders. He said he thought it was fine because I told him to go in the water when he needed to. Apparently I had left out the part about standing waist deep and keeping your shorts on!

I wanted to be mad, mostly because I was embarrassed, but it's hard to be mad when your kids think they're doing the right thing. Children need parents, teachers, and other adult influences so they develop the qualities necessary to be productive adults who don't urinate in public. If they're never taught, these funny kids will turn into law-breaking, social misfits.

It's easy for us to understand this principle when talking about raising kids, but we sometimes miss it when talking about development in other areas. The truth is that we will never succeed until we first build a solid foundation of quality characteristics in our lives. We may function and even accomplish some things of significance, but we will never fully be who we were created to be. This necessary foundation, built with the bricks of interlocking qualities, is what can be defined simply as character.

Character, as defined by dictionary.com, is *the aggregate of features and traits that form the individual nature of some person or thing.*[26] Character is the foundation of your life upon which you make decisions, set direction, and plan for the future. It is who you really are, since we always act according to our character. What you believe dictates what you will do, and what you believe is determined by the elements that make up your character. This is why instilling the right qualities in our kids is essential. We will never be able to make all of their decisions, but if their character is right, then their decisions will be right as well.

This is exactly why leaders and aspiring leaders need to understand both the value and the elements of good character. Leaders are faced with thousands of decisions over the course of their journey, and the quality of their character will make good decisions and steadfast resolve in the face of adversity possible. This is not to say that a leader of good character will never make a mistake, but that their mistakes will not prevent them from moving forward. Whether they win or lose, the right character will keep them focused on the goal of *taking people from where they are to where they need to be.*

Understanding the importance of character in the life of a leader is one thing, but understanding the elements of good character is something else. Many people will tell you how you should act and what you should do as you lead. Remember that this is not about a technique or a way of leading but about being a leader. *So where do we find the elements that make up the character needed in the life of a leader?*

We talked earlier about the importance of knowing we were actually *created.* If we were created, it stands to reason that we have a design.

A great example of this is a car. Two cars from the same manufacturer are created to function in a particular manner. They will go different places and accomplish different things, but if they are not operated according to the manufacturer's design, they will never be able to accomplish what they were designed to do.

When we consider the components that should be a part of our lives, it is helpful to go back to the Bible—the Creator's manual for living. To better understand these necessary components, we look to the New Testament book of Second Peter.

So what is the manufacturer's design for our lives? When we have a question about our car, the first place we look for an answer is in the manual provided by the manufacturer. We can do the same, looking to the Bible to answer the question, "What elements did God intend to be part of MY design?"

The Apostle Peter is an interesting character in the Bible. There is no better example of someone who went from success to failure and back to success. When Peter comes onto the scene of the New Testament, he is an ordinary man working hard to provide for his family. There is nothing truly remarkable about him. Jesus found him while he was fishing and called him to begin fishing for men. Jesus pulled him into the inner circle of disciples and for about three and a half years taught Peter how to find those who did not have a relationship with their Creator and lead them into one. He went from common to extraordinary when the Creator began to personally invest in his life.

Peter infamously denied Christ at a turning point in human history, as Jesus was being tried and sentenced to death on the cross. In a moment of crisis, Peter's character caused him to run away from God instead of to Him.

There was something about facing his own failure that caused Peter's character to change after the Resurrection. It changed so much, in fact, that the first major moment in church history happened as he preached, the result of which was thousands of people entering into a relationship with Jesus. Although not much is known about the later years of the Apostle Peter, history tells us that he was probably martyred for preaching and teaching about Christ. Amazingly, many believe that Peter died by crucifixion, asking to be crucified upside down because he felt unworthy to be killed the same way his Savior was.[27] Peter was a man who underwent a transformation of character that allowed him to be who he was uniquely created to be.

Peter lays out the necessary components of this kind of character in Second Peter 1. He felt strongly that God creates all people for His purpose, as he states in verse 10: "...*give diligence to make your calling and election sure: for if ye do these things, ye shall never fall."* Peter is literally saying, "God has a plan for your life; He has called you and prepared you to do something unique. In fact, before the world was even formed, God knew what He wanted you to do. Be diligent to develop a character based on the things I have told you so that you can fulfill that purpose."

Peter wasn't saying life would always be great if you have these things. This was not a wealth and prosperity message. Peter, and many of those reading these words, gave their lives in pursuit of God's plan. What he was saying was very important: we can expend our lives in the very thing for which we were created if we understand the necessary components of a strong character and then work to make those qualities present in our lives. Coming from the man who notoriously denied that he knew Christ and then later helped thousands come into a relationship with Him, these are powerful words. Peter had finally figured it out, and he wanted others to know as well.

So what are these elements of character that equip us to fulfill our life purpose? We see them listed in verses 5-8 of Second Peter:

> *And beside this, giving all diligence, add to your faith virtue; and to virtue knowledge; And to knowledge temperance; and to temperance patience; and to patience godliness; And to godliness brotherly kindness; and to brotherly kindness charity. For if these things be in you, and abound, they make you that ye shall neither be barren nor unfruitful in the knowledge of our Lord Jesus Christ.*

As we look at each of these individually, begin to take inventory of your own life so you can develop in each of these areas.

Virtue

If I were to develop a list of qualities essential for leadership, I think I might start with courage and resolve. It's amazing to me that this is exactly where Peter begins. The first trait he lists is virtue, defined as "courage, fortitude, resolution; moral excellence."[28] What makes this more remarkable is an understanding of his history. He was a man known for being extremely bold. He spoke his mind and was not afraid to confront others when necessary. We are even told that he cut off the ear of a young man who was with the soldiers the night Jesus was arrested and tried.

But when the pressure was really on, he ran away. As the scene of Jesus' crucifixion began to unfold, Peter lacked the courage, fortitude, and resolve to boldly stand with him. Instead, when questioned about his relationship to Christ, he stated that he didn't know him. I wonder if Peter reflected on that night as he was preparing this letter, wishing that he had demonstrated greater courage.

A leader must have the courage, fortitude, and resolve to do what needs to be done even when it feels like the world is against them. *Taking people from where they are to where they need to be,* doing what is right regardless of the cost requires tremendous courage.

Virtue also means "moral excellence." We might use the word *Integrity* here and understand this as the quality that will cause someone to stand strong for what is right. A morally excellent life, one that pursues those things that are pure, has the freedom to be courageous because it is not bound by the impurities of life that keep so many enslaved. Hebrews 1:2 puts it this way: *"...let us lay aside every weight, and the sin which doth so easily beset us, and let us run with patience the race that is set before us."* Impurity becomes a chain wrapped around us and a weight that holds us down; it prevents us from running the race in front of us. Many courageous leaders have failed because they lacked the moral excellence necessary to lead. When joined with a morally excellent life, courage, fortitude, and resolve become an unstoppable force.

Knowledge

Sometimes a definition is really helpful. At a time like this, not as much. This word commonly means "to know."[29] Knowledge is so important that Peter mentions it right after virtue but doesn't answer the question, "What is it that we need to know?"

First Peter 3:15 helps us understand Peter's intent: *"…be ready always to give an answer to every man that asketh you a reason of the hope that is in you with meekness and fear:"* He is telling the church that they should know why they believe what they believe and be able to explain it to others. While there are a lot of interesting things found in this statement, one of the most interesting is Peter's belief that unbelievers would look to believers and wonder why they were so hopeful!

As he surveyed the culture of his time, he concluded that one of the things lacking was hope. He looked at a world trying to make sense of all the chaos around them and knew that when people without hope encountered those who had it, they would want to know why. And when they were asked, he instructed, they'd better have a clear answer.

This is why knowledge is so important. Peter was not interested in false hope or in a hope based on something that couldn't be explained, but a hope that made sense to those who didn't have it. He was saying to these folks, "You have to know why you have hope and be able to communicate to others why they should have it too." That is the knowledge he refers to in this list—a personal understanding of hope in a hopeless world.

What did they need to know to have this kind of hope? They needed to know at a heart level that their circumstances do not define them, that past hurts and failures do not determine their future direction. They needed to know that, even though they may be terrified, as described in verse 14, they can still confidently move forward. They needed to know that they have a Creator and that He has a plan and purpose for their lives. They needed to understand that His plan is not dictated by their current situation and that their future isn't either, that their goal is to fulfill the purpose for which they were created. They needed to know all of this and be able to explain it to others. This knowledge could not be a knowledge found in the head only, but a knowledge that moved to the heart and became an essential component of their character. With this kind of knowledge, a leader will remain undaunted when life gets out of control.

Temperance

Temperance is a word we don't use much anymore. Simply defined, it means "self-controlled."[30] There is a real lack of self-control in this world. The mantra, "If it feels good, do it," seems to be the pervasive thought of the day. Self-control, or personal discipline, however, is essential to the character of anyone who wants to fulfill his or her created purpose. In First Corinthians 9:25-27 the Apostle Paul puts it this way:

And every man that striveth for the mastery is temperate in all things. Now they do it to obtain a corruptible crown; but we an incorruptible. 26 I therefore so run, not as uncertainly; so fight I, not as one that beateth the air: 27 But I keep under my body, and bring it into subjection: lest that by any means, when I have preached to others, I myself should be a castaway.

When I was in college, a number of my friends were on the college wrestling team. They were all unique (you would have to be a little different to go out in public wearing a singlet), but I always admired their incredible self-discipline. Before a match they would undergo a period of cutting weight that typically involved some pretty extreme measures—a lot of exercise, a steam room as well as starving and dehydrating themselves to the point of near exhaustion. The incredible amount of discipline necessary to win a match is amazing. And they did it, as Paul explained, for something as temporary as a medal.

Paul states that those who strive for something of eternal value need to show the same level of discipline. They need to demonstrate the same level of self-denial so that they can accomplish all they set out to accomplish. He even says in verse 27 that he was worried he'd lose everything he'd worked for without that level of discipline.

Think about this in the context of leadership. If self-control or temperance is not a part of the character of the leader, they will never be able to *take people from where they are to where they need to be.* Without discipline, the leader will not stick with the task long enough to see the goal fulfilled. The leader must be willing to do hard, uncomfortable work with the goal always on their mind. Leadership is about doing what is best for those you lead, regardless of personal cost or discomfort. Work to make personal discipline a part of your character, and you don't have to fear, as Paul did, that your lack of temperance will cause you to lose the things you value most.

Patience

For this definition we look directly to the *Complete Word Study Dictionary:*

> *A bearing up under, endurance to things or circumstances. This contrasts with the type of patience that speaks to long-suffering or endurance toward people. Patience is associated with hope and refers to that quality of character, which does not allow one to surrender to circumstances or succumb under trial.*[31]

The definition alone highlights the importance of patience. A leader does not evaluate whether he's going to continue based on how difficult something may be or how poorly he is received by others. The leader's character must cause him to continue even when others quit.

On May 18, 1780, an event took place that would become known as New England's "Dark Day". For a reason unknown at the time, the skies in New England and part of Canada became so dark that candles were needed for light in the middle of the day. At a time when most natural phenomena were seen as either the blessing or cursing of God, many thought the dark skies signaled His return. In Connecticut, a member of the Governor's council named Abraham Davenport became notorious for his response to his colleague's motion to adjourn their meeting and go home: "I am against adjournment. The day of judgment is either approaching, or it is not. If it is not, there is no cause for an adjournment; if it is, I choose to be found doing my duty. I wish therefore that candles may be brought."[32]

The leader, guided by his character, will allow nothing to prevent him from doing what he has been created and equipped to do.

Godliness

The word translated here as godliness comes from a Greek word that means devotion or piety toward God.[33] This means that we must live in a way that pleases our Creator. When we understand the relationship between the Creator and the leader, it becomes clear that living to please the Creator should be the highest goal of our lives. So many people are confused about the will of God and His ultimate purpose for their lives, but the mystery goes away when our primary goal is to please Him.

The Old Testament book of Ecclesiastes was written by Solomon, the wisest man who ever lived. Solomon lived life in such a way that he could say he had experienced everything. Ecclesiastes points out the futility of so many of life's pursuits when pursued outside of the bigger purpose of God's will. He ends Ecclesiastes with this strong statement in 12:13: *"Let us hear the conclusion of the whole matter: Fear God, and keep his commandments: for this is the whole duty of man."* There is no higher purpose or calling than to live for God and do what He tells us to do in Scripture.

This may be difficult for some to accept, but it is impossible to separate the Creator's plan for our lives from the Creator Himself. While the specific things God desires each of us to do are different, the underlying principle, the thing that should guide both our thoughts and our actions, is the same. Please God by doing what He says. Godliness is being consumed with living in such a way that our Creator will be pleased by how we invested our days on this earth. Ecclesiastes 12:14 ends the previous thought by saying, *"For God shall bring every work into judgment, with every secret thing, whether it be good, or whether it be evil."* An essential part of a leader's character, the element that holds the rest together, is godliness.

Brotherly Kindness

Brotherly kindness is a self-defining term. It literally means one who loves his brother.[34] Since our next chapter will be dealing with this at length, I won't spend a lot of time on it here. Peter is saying that a desire to be connected to others on the same path is an essential part of a right character. Since loneliness and isolation are the enemies of every leader, brotherly kindness, a love for those with the same heart and goals, is absolutely necessary.

Charity

Charity, translated from the Greek "agape," simply means love.[35] This love is the selfless decision to do what is best for others. Love is often misunderstood today. Much of what passes for love is nothing more than an emotional response to someone or something that brings us pleasure. We love people or we love things because of what they do for us or how they make us feel. This love, though, has nothing to do with emotion. This love is not based on how you feel but on a decision you make. Emotion may follow, but it is not the foundation upon which the decision to love is made.

The clearest example of this is Jesus Christ. We are told in the most well-known verse in the Bible that Jesus came to earth because of love. John 3:16 says, *"For God so loved the world that He gave His only begotten Son, that whosoever believeth in Him should not perish but have everlasting life."* Jesus, God in the flesh, left heaven and came to earth to be murdered by His creation, paying the price for sin with His sacrifice. He didn't do this because it felt good; He did it because His love caused Him to do what was best for us.

In Ephesians 5:25, husbands are told to demonstrate this kind of Christ-like love for their wives. *Why?* Because Christ-like love, the "agape" Peter spoke of, is the kind of love that causes one to do what is best for others even when great personal sacrifice is required. When we say that a leader *takes people from where they are to where they need to be*, we can see why love is so important. It is love that will cause the leader to decide to do what is best for those he leads, knowing that a commitment to lead will require sacrifice. Love decides to do what is best for others instead of pursuing an agenda that is best for the one making the decision. It allows for leadership instead of manipulation because it's all about the one being led and not the one leading.

It's not an accident that charity is the last element of character on this list. It is the quality of self-sacrifice and others-mindedness that makes the rest possible. Love paves the way for the leader who works to *take others from where they are to where they really need to be.*

Character is who we are. It informs our decisions and determines not only how we will interact with others, but also whether we will still be around when things get hard. For the leader, understanding not only the importance of character but also its necessary elements is essential. But none of this will matter without a commitment to building these elements into your life. We all have a character. It is the essence of who we are. *Does your character equip you to lead or hold you back?* Make a commitment to develop the character in your life that will allow you to be all that you've been called and created to be.

Discussion Questions

1. Define character. How does that serve as the foundation for life?

2. What element of character listed in the chapter is the greatest challenge to you? Why?

3. Define godliness. How should this impact your life? Does it?

4. How does our character inform the decisions we make?

5. How does Christ demonstrate the power of right character?

Chapter 6

Have the Right Checkpoints

> *"And having thus chosen our course, without guile, and with pure purpose, let us renew our trust in God, and go forward without fear, and with manly hearts..."* [36]
>
> **- Abraham Lincoln**

As mentioned earlier, I had the opportunity, along with 30,000 other members of the First Marine Division, to participate in the invasion of Iraq in March of 2003. As any student of military history understands, in order for a military operation to be successful, particularly when moving an entire division into a country, a tremendous amount of coordination and practice is necessary. For weeks before the actual invasion, unit leaders would get together and do walk-throughs on giant terrain models designed to simulate the battlefield. The lanes that each unit would drive in and the markers that would designate those lanes were carefully memorized so that in the confusion of combat everyone would know what to do.

The good thing, at least from my perspective, was that we were supposed to do this movement during the day so that visibility would not be a problem. We would be driving through mine fields, so knowing that we would be able to see the lane markers in daylight brought great comfort.

And then, as is often the case in war, things changed. Our planned daylight attack started twelve hours earlier than we had planned. This meant that we would be crossing the berm between Kuwait and Iraq at about midnight instead of the next morning. And to make matters worse, our first objective was an oil field that had been set on fire, putting so much smoke into the air that our night vision goggles (NVG) would not work! With no ambient light because of the smoke in the air and without our NVG's, we could only see about twenty feet in front of our vehicles. Nearly zero visibility and we were moving an entire battalion of Marines, more than 1,200, through a minefield with routes and link-up points we couldn't see but were essential to our success.

This is where all of the training and walking around on giant terrain models paid off. Maybe we weren't attacking in the daylight as we had planned, but because we had designated specific checkpoints along our route BEFORE we started moving, we were able to make an extremely difficult and dangerous movement without incident. We could not see very far in front of us, but we knew when we came to a checkpoint or lane marker that we were in the right place. A lot of strange things happened that night, but even with all of the chaos around us, in a place where none of us had ever been, not one Marine got lost and not one vehicle drove into the minefield lining the safety of the designated lanes.

In order for leaders to stay on course, there must be some pre-designated checkpoints along the way. Leadership, just like combat, will get confusing, and we will find ourselves overwhelmed. Our best plans will fall to the wayside as we encounter obstacles and darkness that we never planned for. The truth is, when *taking people from where they are to where they need to be,* if the leader does not have some checkpoints that will keep him on track, he will drift into the minefield of doubt, discouragement and disappointment. It's important to know where you're going, but when you lose sight of the goal, it becomes essential to have some markers that will tell you that you're still traveling in the right direction.

So what are these markers? I am sure there are a number of things that we could say are important in the life of a leader. I have learned, though, that four specific things are non-negotiable in the life of someone who wants to serve others by taking them where they need to go. These serve as the markers that keep a leader on the right path because when any of these fall away, the leader will know that he is in danger. Just as the lane markers brought comfort to us as we tried to avoid the land mines during the first night of the war in Iraq, these markers can provide great comfort to the leader moving through the many obstacles and pitfalls that life can present.

Read

The first checkpoint on the path of leadership is the checkpoint of time in the Bible. I am always amazed and a little bit confused when I have conversations with people who have no idea how to function in life. I'm not surprised when they are concerned with, or struggling to understand, the big issues or how to deal with things that will profoundly impact the future. What amazes me is when the most basic life skills, things like kindness and consideration for others, making decisions with the future in mind instead of simply living in the moment, and how to function within a relationship, are not understood. It is amazing to me because, contrary to what many will say, there is a guidebook that tells us how to do all of these things!

King David put it simply in Psalm 119:105: *"Thy Word is a lamp to my feet and a light to my path."* God's Word, the Bible, is intended to serve as the lamp that lights the path of life so that we don't have to stumble from one bad decision to the next. And yet I have been told again and again that using the Bible as a guide for life is just too simplistic or that the Bible, although not bad, is not relevant.

One ability that I have always wanted to have is the ability to repair cars. In my opinion, mechanics are the closest things to real-life magicians that you can find working outside of Las Vegas! They have the ability to listen to the engine of a two-ton vehicle with its thousands of seemingly unrelated parts and not only know what is broken, but know what needs to be done to fix it! I have never been able to do this. I operate under the "hope" method of vehicle care and maintenance—just keep driving and hope that nothing bad happens!

I am really impressed with those who take old vehicles that aren't working and restore them to the point where they look and operate as well as they did when they originally rolled off of the assembly line. It's great to see a seventy-year-old vehicle working the way it was designed to work more than a generation ago. Apart from the skill involved in restoring such a vehicle, there is a critical component that makes the whole thing possible; the one doing the restorer must understand is the creator's original intent.

Understanding intent in the day of the Internet is easy because obtaining the original owners manuals or specification sheets is as simple as doing a search. *Can you imagine a mechanic looking for the owner's manual for a vehicle that he wants to restore getting upset because the original owner's manual was too simple or no longer relevant?* That would be ridiculous! When you want to make something work the way that it was designed, you look for the manual, the directions produced by the Creator. Otherwise, the best you can do is guess.

I'm afraid that when it comes to life and leadership this is exactly what is happening. Since so many have decided that the manual given to us by the Creator is outdated or irrelevant, they are stumbling through life just hoping that they will happen upon the right answers to the questions they face every day. The leader who is serious about *taking people from where they are to where they need to be* will also be serious about spending time in the owner's manual of life, the Bible. It is in the Bible that we can learn the Creator's intent and begin to understand the way He wants us to live.

There are so many voices in this world trying to get our attention and telling us what to do. *How can we possibly maintain our focus and consistently make the right decisions?* By going back to the source and aligning our lives with the principles given to us by God. Daily time in the Bible is one checkpoint that a leader can use to determine that he is on the right path.

Pray

The second checkpoint is regular time in prayer. One of the most incredible things about God is the fact that we can have a relationship with Him. There are many who view God as unknowable and impersonal. They may believe in God and even, perhaps, believe that He has a purpose or intention for their lives; they just don't believe they can have a relationship with Him. Others would say that they can have a relationship but never experience all that having that relationship really means. They don't talk to God in prayer and so they miss the opportunity to intimately know their Creator.

It can often be difficult for us as finite beings to understand why an infinite God would want to hear what we have to say. The book of Hebrews 4:16 tells us this: *"Let us therefore come boldly unto the throne of grace, that we may obtain mercy, and find grace to help in time of need."* I love this verse because it is not a suggestion! Any doubt that we may have that God wants to hear from us is removed in these few short words. We are not only told to come in prayer, we are told to come boldly!

The imagery here is something with which any parent is familiar. My children have no problem asking me for things. In fact, they'll ask me for things they know they probably won't get, but they ask because they figure they have nothing to lose. If they really want or need something, they will search me out to talk about it regardless of what I might be doing. It is a funny thing as a parent because often the things they are so concerned about would not normally be that important to me. Because my kids are asking, though, I'll stop what I'm doing to meet their need. I love them and want what is best for them and will do what I can to take care of them. Sometimes that means saying, "No," or, "Not right now," but I am thankful that they come to me for help.

God, as our Father, is the same way. We are told in John chapter 3 that when we accept the gift of salvation offered by God through Christ we are born into His family. John 1:12 puts it this way: *"But as many as received him, to them gave he power to become the sons of God, even to them that believe on his name."* We are God's children, and God wants to hear from His kids just as an earthly father would!

Sometimes we don't talk to God in prayer because we feel like we don't deserve anything from Him. It's true that we don't deserve anything from God, but what we deserve is not the point. If we look again at the verse from Hebrews, we are told that we go to God boldly to obtain both grace and mercy in our times of need. We could write volumes of books just dealing with those two words and probably never fully understand the depth of either one. What we can understand, though, is that we are not being told to come and pray for things we deserve.

Grace is the unmerited favor of God. It is God giving to us what we do not deserve but that only He can provide. We see this at work in salvation and throughout our lives with Him. He does not want to give us what we deserve; He wants to bless us out of His heart of love.

Mercy is the other side of the coin. Mercy is God withholding from us what we do deserve. In salvation it means withholding the penalty for our sin and instead applying the righteousness of Christ in its place. Beyond salvation it is our heavenly Father expressing His love and care for us even when we find ourselves in situations that are the result of our own bad decisions or self-will. It does not mean that the consequences for those decisions go away, but it does mean that those circumstances will not separate us either from His love or His plan for our lives. I am thankful when my children come to me, even when it's to ask for help dealing with a bad situation of their own design. God feels the same way about us.

As leaders, we must spend time in prayer asking God for direction and wisdom as we lead, simply sharing both our heart and our struggles. God is our father and wants to hear from us as His children. Even Christ as He lived on this earth would spend time daily talking to God the Father. *Are you in daily prayer?* The answer to that question will serve as a good indication of whether or not you are on the right path leading and living the right way. Talk to your Father; He wants to hear from you!

Fellowship

The third checkpoint that will keep us on track is fellowship with other like-minded individuals. It is important that those we fellowship with share both our goals and a worldview similar to our own, and we absolutely must have them in our lives. It is amazing how easily we can become detached from the reality of the world around us in our daily living. While we would probably never say it, we begin to feel like we are the only ones who struggle and the only ones who have to deal with the daily challenges of life. It is only when we have regular contact with others traveling the same path that we are able to maintain a firm grasp on the reality of our situation. Just as isolation will cause us to lose sight of our purpose and goals, connection with others, if they are the right others, will provide the encouragement and motivation to continue on even when things are difficult.

There were many times as our battalion of Marines drove north through southern Iraq toward Baghdad that I felt overwhelmed by everything that was happening. It's crazy how lonely you can feel when you're constantly around thousands of other people doing exactly the same thing as you, but it does happen. Particularly at night. When it would get dark I often felt as though I was the only person struggling with the loneliness and uncertainty of our environment. I know that my feelings weren't a good filter for the truth, but that's how I felt. Which is why I would walk around and talk to the other Marines in my platoon or go back to the battalion command vehicle whenever I had the chance. I wanted to be an encouragement to others, but I found that as I had conversations and tried to encourage others, the anxiety and loneliness that I often experienced would go away. I had to fellowship with others who were dealing with the same things I was dealing with in order to get the clarity I needed to keep going. I think we can all relate.

Thankfully, our Creator not only understands our strengths but our weaknesses as well. Knowing that we need fellowship and connection with others traveling the same path as us, He provided the institution of the local church to meet that need. I realize that talking about the importance of the local church in a book intended for leaders will seem out of place to many. I've heard the arguments and find that those leading are often the ones who make those arguments most forcefully. There are those who say that the church is for followers and not for leaders. Others say that, as leaders, they just don't have time for the church. Many point to the flawed leaders who have come out of the church and those who have been hurt as a result. The hyper-spiritual say that we don't need the church to worship God, and still others say that they just can't find a church that meets their needs.

Perhaps, in a future book, I will address each of these arguments individually and point to examples both biblical and personal that illustrate their flaws. For the sake of this book, though, let me make a very clear statement that I believe, based on scripture, to be 100% true: If you are trying to lead but are not an active part of a local church, you are not the leader that God created you to be! Said another way, you must be attending and serving in a Christ-centered, Biblically sound fellowship of believers, or you are living outside of God's intention for your life. I know that there are many who will disagree with this, and I know many good people who are leading but are not an active part of a local church. Neither of those changes the truth, though. It is impossible to read the New Testament and not conclude that we are supposed to be an active part of a local assembly.

Consider the following: Jesus traveled and fellowshipped with a group of people throughout His earthly ministry. These were not, as is sometimes thought, only the twelve. There were many disciples or followers who traveled with Him during His three years of ministry prior to crucifixion. Following the resurrection and ascension of Christ to heaven, we see more than 100 people gathered together waiting to see what would happen (Acts 2). What happened was an outpouring of the Holy Spirit that led to more than 3,000 being "added" to the church. It is not a stretch to say that the church started with Jesus and his followers, became 120 gathered in an upper room, and grew into more than 3,000 by the end of Acts 2.

And then, throughout the rest of the New Testament we find instructions for the church, letters to the church, and the establishing of local congregations. These are not, as some may argue, references to a universal church, but local congregations holding services around the world. And then, as things were becoming difficult for these local congregations, the writer of Hebrews says this in Hebrews 10:25: *"Not forsaking the assembling of ourselves together, as the manner of some is; but exhorting one another: and so much the more, as ye see the day approaching."* Not only should we gather together, but we should also get together more often as the day of Christ draws closer! Again, a full discussion on the local church and its importance would take up more space than we have here, but even with these few illustrations we should easily understand that it is God's intention that we are involved in a local, active body of believers.

For the leader, active involvement in the church is non-negotiable. It is in the church that we are reminded that the world is bigger than us. We can hear the Bible preached and through the work of the Holy Spirit experience both conviction and encouragement as needed. We find places of service outside of our established comfort zone and have a place to invest our financial resources that will produce eternal dividends. All of this, and we have the privilege of being a part of the institution established by Christ for the purpose of equipping believers to reach the world! Fellowship is absolutely essential for the leader who has given his life to *taking people from where they are to where they need to be.*

Contact

The final checkpoint is accountability from someone that cares about you personally and has been given the right to speak into your life. I will deal with this specifically in a later chapter, but the need for accountability must be mentioned here as a necessary checkpoint in the life of a leader. Accountability is not something that will come looking for you, but is something that you cannot live without if you are going to be an effective, long-term leader. So many people start well and finish poorly because they have never invited anyone into their life who will tell them the hard truths and get them back on track when they begin to fall away. How many people, after a series of bad decisions, finally stop long enough to reflect on their lives and ask the simple question, "How in the world did I get here?"

One answer is that they didn't have anyone in their life who would hold them accountable. Something must be understood here: If you do not have accountability in your life, that is no one's fault but your own. You can't blame others for not confronting you when things begin to go sideways in your life and leadership. Until you intention- ally find and give permission to the right people, you will not have the kind of accountability that you need. This checkpoint, regular contact with those who care about you and can speak into your life is a checkpoint that you need to re-visit often. In the chapter titled "Include Others" we will deal with this topic more fully, but this checkpoint must be visible on the path of the person who seeks to lead.

Predetermined checkpoints on the path of life and leadership will keep us moving forward when things begin to get difficult and confusing. Leadership is needed most when life seems upside-down, but it is exactly that environment that takes leaders out. By establishing those non-negotiable checkpoints in your life before things get crazy, you will be okay when they inevitably do.

On that dark night in Iraq back in 2003, we met with success because we knew what we were looking for and the exact checkpoints that would tell us we were in the right place. We could have gone for a while just based on passion and will, but eventually, we would have taken a wrong turn and hit a land mine with devastating effects. Maybe you're doing fine now without these four checkpoints. My advice: Establish them in your life before you take another step. Those who lead for a lifetime are those who are committed to the checkpoints of Bible reading, prayer, fellowship, and contact. What you do in those four areas may be the difference between finishing well and not finishing at all.

Discussion Questions

1. What purpose does having predetermined checkpoints in your life serve?

2. Of the four checkpoints listed in the chapter, which ones are a part of your life and which ones are not?

3. Why is regularly reading the Bible an essential checkpoint in the life of a leader?

4. How does fellowship with other like-minded people keep us on the right path?

5. When should you establish these checkpoints in your life?

Chapter 7

Include Others

> *"Brotherhood is the very price and condition of man's survival."* [37]
>
> **- Carlos P. Romolo**

> *"Two are better than one; because they have a good reward for their labour. For if they fall, the one will lift up his fellow: but woe to him that is alone when he falleth; for he hath not another to help him up."*
>
> **- Ecclesiastes 4:9**

There were many things that influenced my early desire to pursue a career in the military. I grew up in a very patriotic family, and some of my extended family members had served in previous wars. Oddly, though, one of the greatest influences was an old book my dad gave me. The book had been his when he was a kid, and somehow he held on to it long enough to give to me when I was nine or ten years old.

The book is titled "They Met Danger" and was written by Gordon Shirreffs in 1960. It's a patriotic collection of short stories about men who have been awarded the Congressional Medal of Honor. This book wasn't the only reason I became a Marine, but it inspired me to consider a life of service. As I read these stories I came to understand how one man's courage can change the outcome of a bad situation.

Later, when I was training to become a Marine Officer at Officer Candidates School, one of the instructors would often pull out what he called "The Bible." It wasn't the Bible I was familiar with, but it was inspiring. It was a volume of citations for every Medal of Honor recipient up to that date. Just as I had while reading "They Met Danger" as a child, I would sit and listen to the instructor read those citations and hope that someday I would demonstrate the same degree of courage and dedication.

Since that time I have heard or read most of the stories of those Medal of Honor recipients, and I am always humbled by the willingness that some people have to put themselves in harm's way for the benefit of others. In fact, more Congressional Medals of Honor have been awarded to someone for throwing their body on a hand grenade than for any other single action. While there are many other amazing and courageous acts done in time of war, throwing yourself on a grenade to save the lives of those around you is in a category all its own. Although some have survived this act, most have not.

The decision to jump on a grenade is a decision to trade your life for the lives of others. I've often asked myself the questions, "What would make someone do that, and at what point do they make that decision?" The time between the throwing of a grenade and its explosion is just a few seconds. That's not when the decision to act is made. There just isn't time.

For whatever reason, the answers to those two questions have always been very important to me. Maybe it's because of my admiration for the self-sacrifice of others, or perhaps it has something to do with the possible implications for my own life. Either way, I have spent a great deal of time wrestling to better understand why.

This becomes easier to understand when we examine the early days of an individual's military service. The goal of basic training is to take an individual, strip away their individuality, and build them back up as a member of a team. Everything that is done in the early days of training is to change the focus from "me" to "we." The importance of depending on one another for nearly everything is stressed in classes, living situations, and training exercises. Those who have served will attest to the fact that you will have few friends in life closer than those with whom you served.

This understanding of doing what is best for the team instead of the individual is essential for a military unit to be successful. It allows commanders to make difficult decisions that will undoubtedly cost the lives of some of their soldiers. It causes people to perform incredibly heroic actions for those to the left and right of them in combat. If training is effective, the decision to do what it best for those around you is made long before the enemy throws his grenade. In a sense, the decision to act bravely is made before circumstances require it. And so young men with their entire lives in front of them do what is best for their brothers even if it costs them their lives.

Understanding this has really changed my perspective on the definition of courage. Courage is not doing something difficult for personal gain. There is nothing wrong with that, but it's not courage. That is an act based on self-will. Courage is doing the hard thing because others need you to! It doesn't mean you won't gain personally; it just means that your primary concern is not for yourself, but for those around you.

We could say it this way: courage is the expression of brotherhood! It is an act that flows from a decision to do what is best for those you care about, a decision made before the act is necessary. *Why?* Because brotherhood brings out the best in us and causes us to do things we wouldn't do otherwise. It motivates us to push through hard circumstances and become the best person we can be. Connection with others in a close relationship provides the perspective and clarity we need to see others and ourselves as we really are and to do the right thing when the wrong thing is easier. Brotherhood causes the soldier on the battlefield to act heroically without thinking and will cause leaders in every other area of life to do the same. The truth is this: without the right people in your life, not just friends but true brothers, you will struggle to act courageously when courage is absolutely necessary.

The topic of brotherhood is not often included in discussions on leadership. We have developed an idea that a leader is someone who acts alone. We believe that a leader is the one who stands up when no one else will and has the ability to walk the path of life by themselves. It's true that a leader will stand up when those around them may not. A true leader will also walk alone if that's what's necessary to *take people from where they are to where they need to be.* Living for God should be motivation enough to act courageously and do what is right.

The truth, though, is that even those who stand when no one else will and whose primary motivation is the glory of God are infused with courage when they value and develop the right kind of relationships. When we look at someone who appears to be standing alone, we are not seeing the many people who have given them the strength, encouragement, and education to do so. The idea of a solitary leader who needs no one and can go it alone is a myth with the potential to destroy those who start out with even the best motives. We need people in our lives who can push us and encourage us to be all that God created us to be.

As we look at this topic, it is important to understand the use of the word "brotherhood" to describe these relationships. When I use the word brotherhood it is not my intent to speak only to men. Brotherhood refers to a relationship, whether between men or between women, that is closer than what we might otherwise call friendship. We use the word friend very loosely to refer to those we have a casual (sometimes even virtual) relationship with. Brotherhood speaks of the type of relationship that is unconditional and transcends a workplace, sports team, or even a stage of life. It is based on trust and transparency and does not carry an expiration date. It is the type of relationship described by Jesus in John 15:13: *"Greater love hath no man than this, that a man lay down his life for his friends."*

A First Century Example

Earlier we considered the life of Paul the Apostle and saw how he dealt with the self-doubt that inevitably comes into the life of a leader. He overcame this doubt because he understood who he was in Christ. But another factor was the importance of brotherhood in his life's story.

He did not start well, at least from a Christian's perspective. This was one of the reasons for the self-doubt in his life. He persecuted Christians and did everything in his power to prevent the spread of Christianity. All of that changed in Acts 9 when Paul had a conversion experience while talking with Jesus. He received a vision revealing to him that he would now spread the Christian message (the gospel) and would endure a tremendous amount of persecution as a result.

Paul immediately began to tell others what Jesus had done in his life. But there was a problem. This guy had been working to have Christians killed but now said he was one of them! Not surprisingly, they didn't believe him. Acts 9:26 says, *"And when Saul was come to Jerusalem, he assayed to join himself to the disciples: but they were all afraid of him, and believed not that he was a disciple."* The other Christians believed that he was just pretending to be one of them so he could do them further harm. God had told Paul what he was supposed to do, but because of his bad reputation, he found himself effectively finished as a minister.

Thankfully, verse 27-28 record this:

"But Barnabas took him, and brought him to the apostles, and declared unto them how he had seen the Lord in the way, and that he had spoken to him, and how he had preached boldly at Damascus in the name of Jesus. And he was with them coming in and going out at Jerusalem."

Paul could not do anything until a man named Barnabas stood up and vouched for him. Barnabas told the other believers about Paul's conversion and took responsibility for his future actions. And just like that, Paul was accepted. Barnabas acted as a brother to Paul and allowed him to begin the journey of service to which he had been called. But their relationship didn't end there.

Shortly after Paul found acceptance with the disciples, he went away by himself to the island of Tarsus. Little is understood about this move, but scholars believe that he lived there for more than ten years following his conversion. Then, in Acts chapter 11, Barnabas traveled to find Paul in Tarsus and bring him back to be with the disciples, acting as a brother and bringing him back to the place God wanted him to be.

As Paul grew in influence and began to travel the world establishing churches and telling others about Jesus, his partner was none other than Barnabas! Barnabas connected Paul to the Christians, re-connected him to his calling, and helped him fulfill that calling. Paul the Apostle changed the world both during his life and after because of his ability to lead others and communicate the truth of the gospel message. Without brotherhood, though, it may never have happened. Paul became the man we talk about today because he understood the importance of having the right relationships.

There is a commonly accepted adage that most people will only have one or two close friends in a lifetime. This may be a bit disheartening, but those who have lived any length of time will acknowledge its truth. Many people will come and go in our lives, but few will fall into the brother category. With that in mind, I want to answer the two questions I am asked most frequently on this topic: "What are the qualities I am looking for in this kind of friend," and, "Where do I find them?"

The Traits of a True Brother

Common Goals and Worldview

We cannot strengthen and encourage another person or be encouraged by them if we aren't going in the same direction. This is why most of us don't have long-term relationships. We have friendships that are based on a job or activity or season of life, and when those things change, so does the relationship. In order to form relationships that transcend the many ups and downs of life, we must share a set of goals and a worldview.

Amos 3:3 says it this way: *"Can two walk together, except they be agreed?"* While agreement on everything is not possible, some key areas of agreement are absolutely necessary for this kind of relationship:

1. A shared worldview. If you believe you were created by a sovereign God who has a plan for your life, and that honoring Him is your highest goal, then those you lean on must share this view. Looking at the world from a Bible perspective impacts the way you think, the things you do, and the way you invest your resources. A true brother will encourage you in the right direction and correct you when you act in a way contrary to a biblical worldview.

2. Agreement on the essential teachings of scripture. While the Bible is God's Word and therefore perfect, the people who read it are not. Good people will always disagree on certain things in the Scriptures. Two people must agree on the essential teachings, however, if they are going to walk the path of life together. If the Bible is to serve as our road map or guide, there must be an in-common understanding of what it says.

3. A gender-specific outlook. Now I know this one may throw you at first, but hear me out. As I mentioned earlier, I do not use the word "brotherhood" to indicate male relationships. I use that word because it connotes something deeper than just friendship. We could also use the word "sisterhood" to describe the same kind of relationship between women, but "brotherhood" is a neutral term to describe this between both men and women. A key point here, though, is that these relationships *are* gender specific. Except for the relationship between husband and wife, the type of relationship we are describing should not be between individuals of the opposite sex.

The reason? There are many, but the biggest one is that men and women view the world differently. We need someone who understands how we look at the world and can speak to us from that place of understanding. In his book "Disciplines of a Godly Man," Kent Hughes says:

Men, if you are married, your wife must be your most intimate friend, but to say, "My wife is my best friend" can be a cop-out. You also need Christian male friends who have a same-sex understanding of the serpentine passage of your heart, who will not only offer counsel and pray for you, but will also hold you accountable to your commitments and responsibilities when necessary.[38]

The same could be said of women. It is essential to have someone in your life who understands what is going on in your heart from their own experience. That way, when they give you advice, encouragement, or direction, they speak to who you are instead of what you pretend to be. You need someone who knows the real you and is not afraid to keep you on the right path.

Mutual Concern

There is a difference between having a counselor and having a friend or brother in your life. In brotherhood there will be times when counsel is given, but that is not the reason for the relationship. The relationship exists so that two people can encourage and strengthen each other as they do the things they have been called and equipped by God to do. A counselor is someone who gives counsel and expects nothing in return. That relationship is not mutual.

The key to having the type of brotherhood relationship we are talking about is being the right kind of brother! I love the way Philippians 2:3-4 explains how we should treat each other: *"Let nothing be done through strife or vainglory; but in lowliness of mind let each esteem other better than themselves. Look not every man on his own things, but every man also on the things of others.*" Express a sincere concern for others and focus on being the right kind of friend instead of having the right kind of friend. This shift from self-focused to selfless makes the rest of this possible.

Transparency and Trust

Without transparency and trust, brotherhood will never be present. It was the transparency and trust between the Medal of Honor recipients and their comrades that allowed them to make the ultimate sacrifice without a second thought. Unfortunately, we in the modern era have lost much of our understanding of what a transparent, honest relationship looks like. Social media allows us to have "friends" and "followers" who know very little about us. These guarded relationships become normal in other areas of our lives, and eventually we have no one who can speak to us at a heart level because we have no one in our lives who knows our heart. We have to understand what transparency really look likes and then be willing to trust that our brothers will use that transparency for our benefit.

The simplest description of the levels of transparency I have found comes from *Why Am I Afraid to Tell You Who I Am?* by John Powell. In this book he outlines what he calls the five levels of communication.[39]

1. Cliché Level. Most of us operate at this level. Picture yourself joining someone in an elevator. It would be awkward to pretend they aren't there, so you look at them, nod, and say, "Hello." If you're really chatty you may ask them how they're doing. Most people will answer with the obligatory, "Fine, thank you," and then your conversation is over. This is the cliché level. Neither of you really cares how the other

is doing, but you go through this process because that is what we do. It has very little, if any, meaning.

2. Fact Level. The fact level is a little bit deeper than the cliché level but not much. Same elevator and same person waiting to finish their ride, but this time you are really feeling like a conversation. Instead of just asking how they're doing, you also comment on the weather. "Sure is hot out today." It is more than cliché because you are stating a fact. But that is all that changes.

What's interesting about the fact is that unlike the cliché, it can be helpful in the right situations. Teachers often teach at this level. They communicate the facts without really telling you what to think about them. Restaurant service staff operate at this level when they answer questions about menu items or costs, as do tellers and clerks and attendants of all kinds. Most of the world operates at the fact level. It can be very helpful but does not serve to build close relationships.

3. Opinion Level. This level requires a degree of trust when used in person-to-person conversation. Many people will give their opinion in a public forum where there is little actual connection to the audience, but trust is required to offer your opinion to someone you care about. You can still be guarded at this level by saying things like, "That's just my opinion," when you think others may not like it. There is very little emotional involvement. This level can be a bit like putting your toe into the swimming pool before jumping in. You say what you think, but no real harm has been done if it doesn't work out.

4. Emotional Level. We begin to reveal what is going on inside us. The emotional level of transparency requires a high degree of trust since, if received wrong, we could be hurt. Beyond simply stating our opinions, we are now expressing how those opinions make us feel.

Most relationships never get to this level, but sharing your emotions with another person is necessary for them to support and encourage you. Interestingly, the mutual concern we looked at earlier is important here. When we know we are sharing our emotions with someone who is also willing to share how they feel about us, the level of trust increases along with the willingness to move to the level of transparency.

5. Transparency Level. Nothing is off the table. Trust has been built to the degree that regardless of what is said the relationship is not in danger. Here we can reveal our heart, both the good and the bad, and help, encouragement, and, when necessary, correction will be offered.

As we look at the people we consider brothers, we need to determine how willing we are to be transparent with them. Transparency requires time to get to know someone, but it is essential if we are going to have others in our lives who will walk with us through both the good and the bad times.

Vulnerability

The last element in this relationship is vulnerability. This is different than transparency, which is the willingness to be completely open and honest. Vulnerability is the willingness to have someone take that transparency and be completely open and honest back. You are putting yourself in a place where someone can tell you the things you don't want to hear, and instead of getting angry you rejoice in the fact that you have that kind of person in your life. It is a lonely existence to hear only the things you want to hear. You experience growth and safety when you hear the things you need to hear.

Vulnerability requires the other characteristics we have mentioned. When we know that our brother has similar goals and worldviews and that we both want to do what God has called us to do, then we know the things they tell us in vulnerability are not meant to hurt us but are meant for our good. Proverbs 27:6 says, "Faithful are the wounds of a friend; but the kisses of an enemy are deceitful." It's a blessing to have someone in your life who loves you enough to tell you the hard things.

Where do I find them?

So where do we find people like this? This is where most people fail in the pursuit of brotherhood. They want to have relationships like this but spend their lives looking for those relationships in the wrong places.

As simple as it sounds, the best place to find this type of person is in the place this type of person likes to go! I know; not very deep. I can't express how frustrating it is for me to have conversations with people who tell me they have no one in their life whom they can depend on. They talk about how hard it is to find the kind of person described above but spend all their time either isolated from the world, making no attempt to meet people, or trying to meet people in places where a person pursuing their God-given purpose would never go.

If you want to find people who will help you become the person you were created to be, find others who are doing the same things you are. These places could be churches, civic groups, or service organizations. Find a place full of people who are living for something bigger than themselves and get to know some of them. Make a deliberate effort to develop relationships with those on the same path as yourself, and you'll be surprised by what happens.

An interesting event took place later in Paul's life that really highlights the power of brotherhood. Paul was an aging man when he was taken as a captive to Rome. Although he was an incredible leader, he had very human moments of discouragement. As he traveled in captivity he must have been tired and lonely and may have even questioned what was happening in his life. In Acts 28 we find this verse: "And from thence, when the brethren heard of us, they came to meet us as far as Appii forum, and the three taverns: whom when Paul saw, he thanked God, and took courage" (vs. 15). When he was able to meet with those he considered brothers, Paul regained his perspective and was filled with courage for the road ahead.

We need to have people in our lives who are closer than friends. We need brothers. "Including others" means that we are not trying to walk this road of life on our own. We need to broaden our circle of friends to include people who can provide the encouragement and direction that we need to lead according to our design. Without them we are missing an essential element in the pursuit of leadership.

Discussion Questions

1. How do you define brotherhood? Who are some people in your life that you would put into this category?

2. In what way does brotherhood inspire courageous actions?

3. Why is transparency important when developing these close relationships?

4. What happens if we do not have these relationships in our lives?

5. What is the goal in a close, "brotherhood" type of relationship?

Chapter 8
Defeat Fear

"In any moment of decision, the best thing you can do is the right thing, the next best thing is the wrong thing, and the worst thing you can do is nothing."[40]

- Theodore Roosevelt

A leader will face many obstacles over the course of their leadership journey, but I believe there is one that is especially common among those who have decided to lead. This has often kept me from fully embracing the roles and opportunities God has given me and caused me to act outside of His purpose for my life. It has a name that we all understand but don't want to admit would ever apply to us. I believe the number one obstacle for any leader is the obstacle of *fear*. As we discussed in chapter 3, it is the God-given purpose of every person to live in a way that glorifies or uplifts Him. The way we do this is by using our specific gifts, abilities, and opportunities to serve others. We are to lead in a way that *takes people from where they are to where they need to be*—not for our own purposes, but because we want what is best for them. Any time we are not fully utilizing those specific gifts, abilities, and opportunities, we are not fully living within our design. We are not all that we could be because we are not all that we were created to be. What a tragedy it is to draw breath and yet never fully live.

Sadly, most people never know what it is to fulfill their potential, even those who look successful from the outside. Some people are just so self-centered that they spend their lives meeting their own needs and fulfilling their own desires. Others are simply following the example that was modeled for them. They would do something different—they just don't know what different is.

I often fall into a third category. I want to make a difference with my life. I know that I have a responsibility to serve others by helping them to get where they need to go. I have been taught right and know that this life thing is bigger than me. But I often have a difficult time leading where I am. Why? I believe that my biggest leadership struggle is accepting that the gifts and opportunities given to me will actually make a difference in the lives of others. I have an often unspoken fear that I am simply not good enough. Sometimes it's clear that I can impact those around me. Other times, though, I let things happen around me without trying to leverage what God has given to lead others forward.

Whether your problem is selfishness, or ignorance, or an insecurity about your own gifts, the net result is the same; things go undone and potential goes unfulfilled because a life is not fully lived. I wonder how many times I could have provided direction and leadership to those God placed in my life but simply did not? I am thankful for the things God has allowed me to be a part of and look forward to many more years of serving Him by serving others. I know that human leadership is fallible and that we cannot always do everything right, but it is still important to evaluate our lives so that we can be the best leaders possible. I don't want to get to the end of my life and find out that I could have done so much more if only I had taken a few minutes to look at both my strengths and shortcomings. As I have considered this area of my life, two verses challenge me to fully be what God has uniquely created me to be.

The Apostle Paul wrote two letters to a young pastor by the name of Timothy. Timothy had traveled extensively with Paul and looked to him as a kind of spiritual father. We are given the impression that Paul taught Timothy how to minister and that Timothy learned so well he would eventually become an important pastor in the first-century church. While Paul may have struggled with pride (he often mentioned his pedigree when writing), Timothy seemed to go the other way. He was obviously talented and loved God, or Paul would not have spent much time with him. Paul was always pushing forward and had little patience for those who were not willing to move at his pace. What we learn from the first few verses of Second Timothy 1 is that he sincerely loved Timothy and wrote these letters to provide both encouragement and direction as he began his ministry as a pastor. Before he gives instruction in this second letter, he gives a personal admonition: "Wherefore I put thee in remembrance that thou stir up the gift of God, which is in thee by the putting on of my hands. For God hath not given us the spirit of fear; but of power, and of love, and of a sound mind" (1:6-7).

This seems a bit out of place and is easy to pass over. For me, though, it jumps off the page. I can only imagine what Timothy was dealing with as a young pastor. He must have been overwhelmed, and even though he was clearly capable, he began to have his doubts about whether he could make a difference. So Paul begins this letter by telling Timothy to fully embrace the person that God had created him to be!

Look at verse 6 again: *"Wherefore I put thee in remembrance that thou stir up the gift of God, which is in thee by the putting on of my hands."* Paul wanted Timothy to remember the time when God made him aware of his unique gift. At some point before these letters Paul had laid hands on Timothy and prayed that God would equip him for the work ahead. And God did! For some reason, though, Timothy was not using that gift as it was intended. Paul told him to stir that gift up, to get it out and use it to its fullest capacity. You see, before Paul could give specific instruction about what needed to be done, he knew that Timothy had to fulfill his potential. He had to lead others the way God had equipped him to lead.

So why did Timothy struggle with this? Look at the next verse: *"For God hath not given us the spirit of fear."* Timothy struggled to leverage his gifts because he was afraid! Now this statement really convicts me. I will acknowledge that I am not always what I should be and that I fail at times to use the gifts God has given me, but to say that I am afraid?

Fear is a funny thing because it looks different in each person's life. There are things you would never do that I would not even think twice about and things that you do that would scare me to death! The reality, though, is that fear, if not recognized and dealt with, can be just as destructive as any other negative behavior when it comes to doing what you are supposed to do.

What's crazy as we look back at this verse is that I don't think Timothy was afraid of people being upset or even of persecution. He was one of Paul's closest traveling companions and had experienced all of that in the past. I think he was afraid that he wasn't good enough or compassionate enough or smart enough to do the work of leading a church. You see, his fear, just like so many of ours, would not have looked like fear from the outside. But it was fear because it was an obstacle keeping him from the path set in front of him by God.

Paul deals specifically with this in the last part of verse 7: "*but of power, and of love, and of a sound mind.*" Paul wanted Timothy to understand that when God gives a gift, he also gives the power, the capacity, and the mental ability to leverage that gift for His purpose! God does not give us gifts without giving us the opportunity to use those gifts as He intended. Fear, when it comes to leveraging our leadership gifts, is a lack of confidence in the One who gave us those gifts. Fear is saying to the One who created us, "I know what you want me to do, I just don't think you've given me everything I need to do it." If God has given you gifts, He will also give you everything that you need to exercise those gifts.

When I fail to use the gifts of leadership God has given me to help others *get from where they are to where they need to be*, I am allowing the fear that I am not strong enough or smart enough or capable enough to keep me from doing what He intended for me. And in those moments I may be drawing breath, but I am not fully living. I am comforted when I read these verses because I realize I'm not the only one who struggles and that God has given me everything I need to be the leader He created me to be.

What about you? Maybe your leadership struggle is different than mine, but whatever is keeping you from leading the way God equipped you to lead is keeping you from being all that you were created to be. Don't let fear, whatever that fear may be in your life, keep you from fulfilling your unique purpose. Defeat fear by trusting the one who created you more than you trust those things that are keeping you from moving forward. What have you been uniquely equipped to do that will go undone if you do not fulfill your God-given purpose?

What is keeping you from *taking the people in your life from where they are to where they need to be?*

Discussion Questions

1. What are some of the obstacles in your life that keep you from leading the way that you know you should?

2. What part does fear play in the leadership obstacles in your life?

3. In what ways do we mask or redefine fear and make it look like something else? Is it possible to make fear, under another name, look like a good thing?

4. What are some ways you defeat fear along your leadership journey?

5. What are some things you haven't done because of fear? How will you change that going forward?

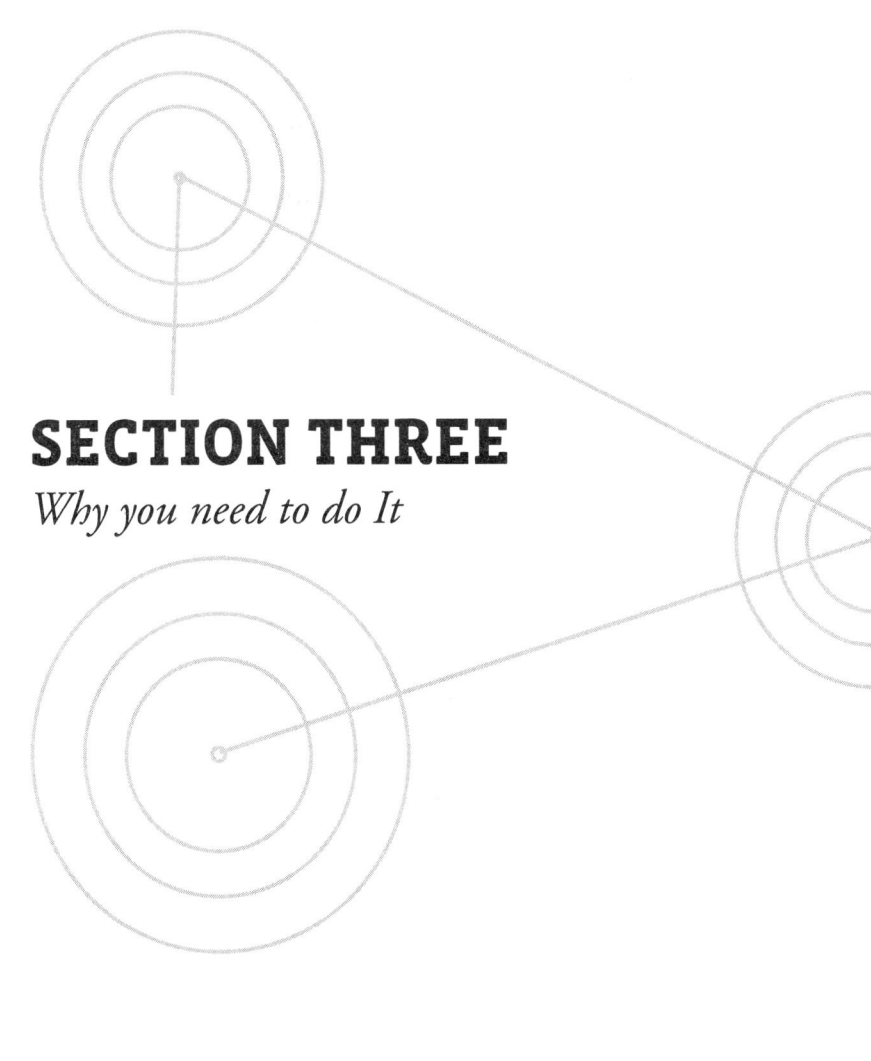

SECTION THREE

Why you need to do It

Chapter 9

The Story of Your Life

> *"Make no little plans; they have no margin to stir men's blood and probably themselves will not be realized. Make big plans, aim high in hope and work. Remember that our sons and grandsons are going to do things that would stagger us."*[1]
>
> **- Daniel Burnham**

One of the greatest joys of my life was and always will be serving in the Marine Corps as a part of the Fifth Marines. I grew up during my time there and learned what it is to really lead. Not too long ago I had the opportunity to re-visit Camp Pendleton, where I was stationed, and in a strange way it felt like I was visiting a childhood home. For me, that time was not just about doing a job; it was about being a part of a big, amazing (and sometimes dysfunctional) family.

When I checked in as a Second Lieutenant I had the opportunity to lead First Platoon, Charlie Company, First Battalion Fifth Marines, and I learned more in just a few months there than during my year of schools. From that platoon I moved to a different company in the same battalion, Weapons Company. For those who are not familiar with the Marine Corps, Weapons Company is where the Marines with the big machine guns and vehicle-mounted anti-armor missiles serve. My platoon was called the Counter-mechanized Platoon and had heavy machine guns, anti-armor missile systems, and eighteen HMMWV's (Hummers). We were two platoons combined into one, which gave us all these weapons systems and vehicles as well as nearly eighty Marines.

While my first platoon taught and grew me, this platoon challenged and stretched me. It's amazing that I made it out of the Marine Corps without being fired and with my reputation (somewhat) intact. A very common scene was me standing in front of my Company Commander trying to explain the behavior of one or more of my Marines and why I thought that behavior was okay. Most of the time I was hearing about the incident for the first time, but somehow I managed to talk my way out of trouble with only a stern warning to get the platoon under control.

The one thing I had going for me was that these guys were amazing in the field. When it came to doing their job, there was not a group of professional infantrymen in the Marine Corps that could match them. I guess that's why I was willing to take the heat for their actions. They may have been barbarians in normal society, but barbarians are exactly who you want when things begin to fall apart. I have always said that I didn't lead the platoon as much as I worked to channel it in the right direction. Thankfully, what was a liability at Camp Pendleton was an incredible asset in war.

As our time in Iraq came to a close and we were preparing to return home, I learned another lesson from these Marines that proved to me they really could act civilized when necessary. The First Marine Division of which we were a part had more than 30,000 Marines and was led by the famed General James Mattis. General Mattis is a student of history and decided that, based on other military campaigns, it would harm the military's image if Marines took home what he called war trophies, which were anything picked up off the battlefield as a souvenir. He felt so strongly about this that he gave an order that the unit of a Marine who tried to take one home would stay back in Iraq until the rest of the division was home. This would mean a delay of at least a few months.

We were all thankful for the opportunity to serve in combat, but we were also looking forward to going home and, for many, leaving the Marine Corps. General Mattis extended his order to include other disciplinary actions that could hold units back. It was amazing to see the behavior change in Marines that had a hard time keeping themselves within the confines of civility. The order to leave souvenirs behind was not a new one, but the accompanying threat was. Waking up the morning after the order was issued we found piles of these war trophies that hours before Marines would have sworn did not exist. Along with that, general behavior changed. No one was perfect (they were Marines after all), but the attitude that getting home was more important than getting in trouble pervaded. For the few weeks between the order and when we boarded a plane for California, thoughts and actions changed to reflect a focus on the future. This is where I first learned the power of living with the end in mind.

Living with the end in mind

I was genuinely concerned when General Mattis gave the order about war souvenirs. I had worked with these Marines for two years and was convinced we would be staying behind. I was proud of them and thankful to be their platoon commander, but they were never going to listen to this one. But they did. (At least they did enough to not get caught. I'm still not convinced they complied, but we all came home on time.) When the focus shifted from what was happening in the moment to what could happen in the future, attitudes changed. There is power in viewing your life from the perspective of what could be instead of what is.

For the leader, this often provides the motivation and the clarity to move forward when things become difficult or foggy. Living with the end in mind gives you the opportunity to plan and act in a way that will move you from where you are to where you desire to be. This process, living with the end in mind, is called *legacy*.

An understanding of legacy cannot be neglected if we are going to be the kind of leaders who live to *take others from where they are to where they need to be.* The type of leadership we have been discussing is not about what we do but about who we are. It is not about a job or some other pursuit that brings temporary fulfillment but about making a difference in the lives of those you can influence. Leadership that understands legacy is leadership that transcends the ups and downs of life because it is not rooted in a moment or a season but in consistently doing the right thing. When we live and lead with the end in mind we will come to the end of our lives thankful to have invested in others instead of broken because we chased after things that didn't matter. We are living to make our life count instead of living only to get what we want.

I like to share two analogies when talking about legacy. The first is the analogy of life found in a book. In a very real way our legacy, how we will be remembered, is the story of our life being written every day. We get up and go about our lives, adding new sentences and, some days, whole paragraphs to the story that will one day be told about us. We know that in any good book there are chapters with twists and turns, ups and downs, and moments of both light and dark. Taken individually these chapters can be confusing and only describe a small part of what is actually happening. When we read the chapters in the right order, though, they tell a compelling story. So it is with our lives. There will be good moments and bad, but no single moment or season accurately reflects the totality of our lives. It is only when all the moments come together that the real story becomes clear.

Figure out what you want your story to be and begin to write those chapters! Many people look at the chapters of their lives that have already been written and lose hope. The great thing about an unfinished story is that at any moment the author can hit the return key on his keyboard and start a new paragraph or a new chapter. It's not over until it's over, as they say, but you must decide how you want it to end. Living each day to write the story you want told when you die is how you leave a legacy that has value beyond the years you spend on this earth.

The second analogy that helps me understand the idea of legacy is the analogy of a gift. Have you ever received a gift that was so valuable that you didn't want to put it down or let anyone else touch it? Or maybe you've received a gift that had no value to you at all. You are too polite to say anything, of course, but the gift has so little value that you throw it in the trash the first chance you get.

Now imagine your legacy as a gift that you are leaving for those coming behind you. People are looking to you for direction, and the gift of your legacy is the direction they will receive. *If you died, and your legacy was put in a box and given as a gift to those who needed it, what would they do with it? Would they be so happy when they looked inside the box that they didn't want to put it down because of the value it would add to their life, or would they throw it away the first chance they got?* Your legacy will either be valuable or worthless depending on how you live today.

Every one of us will leave a legacy. Good or bad, we cannot get away from the fact that how we live today will determine the impact we have on those looking to us for direction in an increasingly difficult world. But how do we leave the kind of legacy we desire? Life is hard, and so much of it is just trying to get by. What do we need to do to live in such a way that our lives count for something bigger than ourselves?

Realize the impact your life has.

One of the major reasons we don't truly live with the end in mind and we don't take this idea of legacy seriously is that we don't really believe the way we live makes a difference. We think we can go about our days and turn those days into years with very little impact on those around us. Here are a few interesting studies to consider:

Children in father-absent homes are almost four times more likely to be poor. In 2011, 12% of children in married-couple families were living in poverty, compared to 44% of children in mother-only families.[42]

A study of 1,977 children age 3 and older living with a residential father or father figure found that children living with married biological parents had significantly fewer externalizing and internalizing behavioral problems than children living with at least one non-biological parent.[43]

71% of high school dropouts are fatherless.[44]

Statistical data showed that a 1% increase in the proportion of single-parent families in a neighborhood is associated with a 3% increase in an adolescent's level of violence.[45]

A study of 109 juvenile offenders indicated that family structure significantly predicts delinquency.[46]

Children with a parent who commits suicide are three times more likely to also take their own life.[47]

Looking at statistics that so clearly reveal the connection between parental involvement and the success of children, it's hard to conclude that the way we behave doesn't impact the people in our lives. Through the work we do at Mighty Oaks, we spend a great deal of time addressing the veteran and active-duty military suicide rate and working with those who have struggled with taking their own lives. The fact that more than twenty veterans and service members decide to take their lives each day is difficult to understand and something we work to change.

As alarming as the rate we're losing men and women who have served this country is, the death of a service member or veteran by their own hand is not the most tragic part. The real tragedy to me is the generational impact a decision to end one's life has. We like to think that the decisions we make have very little impact on those around us or that our family would be better off if we took ourselves out of the picture, but we know this is not true! When someone takes their life, the impact of that decision is felt later when their child or someone close to them eventually does the same. As shown above, children of a person who takes their life are three times more likely to do the same. Potentially, generation after generation of fathers and mothers will take their lives following the example, the legacy, that was left for them. While legacy is about more than simply being a good parent, the conclusion that the way we live affects only ourselves is contrary to the data.

Think through the various relationships in your life and ask the question, "How do the decisions I make today impact the lives of those I am in a position to influence?" Instead of looking at those relationships in terms of what you can get from them, begin to look at them from the perspective of what you can give back. Living with the end in mind is living with the understanding that how I live either encourages or prevents others from getting to where they need to be.

Understand why you were created.

Perhaps you've heard the saying, "He who dies with the most toys wins." The problem with this philosophy is that, toys or not, you still die. It's true that many people use the accumulation of things to measure their success. They stockpile possessions, authority, titles, or influence and use them as a yardstick to compare their success to that of the people around them. This is the reason so many of us allow jobs or hobbies to define us and why we count the days to the weekend, vacation, or retirement. We have adopted the belief that our time on this earth is for us.

Getting this legacy thing right requires that we consider why we were created in the first place. So many people get to the end of their lives and find them empty because they never lived for the purpose for which they were created. We spent an entire chapter on the topic of creation, but I want to add a few things to that discussion.

First, even though our society judges us based on what we consume, we were not designed to consume but to produce. Genesis 1 records the first instruction of God to man: *"And God blessed them, and God said unto them, Be fruitful, and multiply, and replenish the earth, and subdue it"* (verse 28). God's intention for mankind from the very beginning was that we would be fruitful and produce. We could argue that he is speaking about reproduction, but that's not what He says. He includes reproduction ("multiply"), but he starts with being fruitful!

I believe the implication is both specific and general at the same time. God is saying that we need to do something productive with our lives (specific) but did not tell us specifically what that is (general). We are all different and will each follow a different path. Living a life of fruitfulness is far more important than vocation or title. We were created to produce.

Second, the future of our society absolutely depends on us doing what we were created to do. Failure in any area is a failure of leadership. If our homes, communities, companies and churches are going to succeed, men and women are going to have to step into their God-given roles as leaders. Many of us talk about how bad the world around us is becoming without ever considering that the catalyst for change may be us! We were created to serve by providing leadership. In order for future generations to succeed, we need to be willing to move beyond our own desires and begin to *take people from where they are to where they need to be.*

Finally, we need to remember that we're talking about why we as individuals were created, not why everyone else was created. It's so easy to take the principles of leadership and legacy and evaluate how well others are applying them to their lives. But leadership is about the people you lead, not you. The decision to lead, however, is completely about you. Living to leave a legacy and investing your days in leading others is not something that will happen by accident or when everyone else starts doing what they're supposed to do. You were created to do this whether the rest of the world gets in line or not. Do what you were created to do and don't let the attitudes of others get in the way.

Live on purpose.

We naturally drift away from the things we should be doing. Very few people decide that their legacy is going to be one of emptiness and waste, but many people end up there. *Why?* Because even though most of us would say that we want to leave a healthy legacy that impacts generations of people after us, we never live intentionally enough to make it happen.

In his book *The Screwtape Letters,* C.S. Lewis paints this picture of humanity: "Indeed the safest road to Hell is the gradual one—the gentle slope, soft underfoot, without sudden turnings, without milestones, without signposts."[48] I am afraid that many people, even those not on their way to hell, live this way, gradually drifting into a life without impact. If you are going to leave a legacy that matters and impact those who are looking to you for leadership, you must be intentional. *The question is how?*

First, you must decide what you want your legacy to be. *This sounds simple, but how many people have actually taken the time to sit down and write out the things they want to be said about their life when they are gone?* It's been suggested that all of us should write the eulogy we want to be read at our funeral and then live the life that will allow it to be read honestly. As the song says, "Live your life so the preacher won't have to lie at your funeral!"[49] This is not something that can be taken lightly or be done in haste. We are so busy that we often forget to consider where exactly we're going. Spend some time in prayer and ask God through the Holy Spirit that "will guide you into all truth" to make His desire clear (John 16:13). Write down and review often the destination you will point your life toward.

Second, once you have decided in concrete terms what you want your legacy to be, honestly evaluate your life and determine what needs to be added or taken away to accomplish that goal. Maybe you need to add education or training, mentorship or even a different job to get where you believe you should go. Maybe for you it is not addition but subtraction that needs to take place. Friends, habits, and negative perspectives are often the things that keep you from moving forward and need to be removed. Look at your life as objectively as possible and figure out what resources you are lacking to live to your full, God-given potential. Have a trusted friend look at your life and make recommendations. Sometimes an outside perspective is exactly what we need to get things right. Whether it comes from you or someone else, an honest inventory of your life will help you formulate the plan that will get you to your goal.

Third, consider the impact of not living to leave a worthwhile legacy. *Who will be impacted negatively if you forget that life is not about you and live to please yourself instead of living to impact others?* On my desk I have a picture of my wife and a picture of my four children. I love them, but that's not the reason I keep these pictures on my desk. There is very little risk of me forgetting what they will look like since I go home to them every day. I keep these pictures close by because they remind me what is at stake if I don't do what God has created me to do. I need that reminder so that when I feel like living to fulfill my own desires, I can quickly regain the proper perspective.

I know, though, that this legacy thing is bigger than my family. There are friends, an organization, and people that I have yet to meet that will all be impacted if I stop doing what I'm supposed to do. Setting the goal is important, and understanding what needs to be added or taken away from our lives to accomplish that goal is essential.

And when things get hard, we need to have the faces of the people who need us in our minds. *What will go undone if you don't do what you were created to do?*

Finally, as simple as it sounds, you need to go to work! I could write an entire book on all the things I plan on getting to someday. We probably all have lists of things we want to do eventually that, if we are honest, we know will never get done. I remember when our kids were small and it was a fight just to get through each day. People always told us to enjoy those days because they would be over before we knew it. At the time, I was hoping they would be over soon! Someone told us that with children the days may be long but the years are short. What a truth that is. I look at my kids now and wonder where the time has gone.

That's how life works. We are so busy getting by that we never get around to doing the most important things. Once you have determined your direction, don't let anything keep you from beginning to move. You may ask, "Where do I start?" Start where you are. One step at a time, one day at a time, because truly those steps and days become the years that write the story of your life. Go to work!

We are all writing the stories of our lives that will become our legacies. They are stories that began the day we were born and will not end until we take our final breath. I wonder what story your life will tell. *Will it be a legacy that points the way forward when things get tough, or will it be the legacy of a person who decided the best thing to do in the face of hardship was to give up?* The decisions you make today will impact generations of people following you.

One question that clarifies this issue for me is this: *if the people I have the opportunity to influence live their lives the same way I live mine, will they end up in a place I can be proud of?* Live your life in such a way that when your story, your legacy, is put in a box and given as a gift to those coming behind you, they will hold it tight because of its value. Begin to live today with the end in mind!

Discussion Questions

1. What does it mean to "live with the end in mind"?

2. Why do most people live for right now instead of considering the end of their lives?

3. In what ways are you developing your legacy today? Are you proud of the story that your life is writing?

4. What are some things that need to change in your life today so that you can leave the legacy that you want to tomorrow?

5. What is at stake if you do not make the changes you know you should make?

Chapter 10
It's Time

"Reject passivity, accept responsibility, lead courageously." [50]

- Robert Lewis

"Beware of rashness, but with energy and sleepless vigilance, go forward and give us victories." [51]

- Abraham Lincoln

There comes a time in the life of every leader when the discussion ends and the leading begins. It's funny, but for some reason we take a great deal of comfort in talking about something difficult even when we are not really doing the difficult thing. Leading is hard. It is much easier to talk about the need and examine the issue and put a plan together than it is to actually get moving. But when we understand that God created us to lead others, *taking them from where they are to where they need to be,* we can't get around the fact that at some point we're going to have to get started.

After leaving the Marine Corps I began working at the church my family and I had attended while at Marine Corps Base Camp Pendleton, and for the next five years I learned everything I could about full-time ministry. It was not without its ups and downs, but with strong mentorship I believed I was prepared to follow God's leading to become the senior pastor of a church that would soon be without one.

So, in August of 2008 my family and I moved the 430 miles from Oceanside California to the San Francisco Bay Area city of Fremont to begin a new life of ministry. The church wasn't large, but I felt blessed to be able to serve alongside the wonderful people there. As is true when doing anything for the first time, my weaknesses and lack of experience leading a church were evident to me nearly every day. I was thankful for the good things that were happening but overwhelmed with the many decisions I needed to make and the direction I needed to set.

Shortly after our one-year anniversary at the church we hosted a conference with guest speaker Bud Calvert. Pastor Calvert was my pastor for a short time when I was a child and had been my parent's pastor during the years my dad was also a pastor. Pastor Calvert had started an amazing church in Fairfax, Virginia, and because of the many senior military leaders that attended his church, he had a tremendous amount of experience leading leaders. I was thankful he chose to speak at the conference but even more thankful for the time we spent together between meetings. I asked him as many questions as I could think of, and he graciously and patiently answered each one.

One evening as we were having dinner, I told him about some of the challenges I was facing and that I didn't know how to work through all of them. Not wanting to sound dumb, I told him what I thought about each challenge and assigned blame as necessary. I didn't want him to think I was the problem, only that I was trying to figure out how to fix the problems! Finally, I ran out of things to say and stopped long enough to ask Pastor Calvert what he thought.

I honestly expected him to tell me to keep up the good work or to hang in there until things got better. Instead, he told me what I needed to hear. He stopped eating and leaned as close to me as he could from across the table. "You need to lead", he said. I didn't know how to respond to that, so he explained that there wasn't one problem I had shared with him that couldn't be fixed if I was willing to show the way forward. What he was saying, very clearly I might add, was that the time for talk and examination was over. It was time to start doing what I knew I should do! It was time for me to take responsibility and do what I was there to do-lead.

That conversation changed so many things for me. I don't get it right all the time, but I have come to understand that it's not my job to simply point out the problems or talk about the issues. My job is to make the best decisions I can and then get up and lead. It's been said that the most wasted resource in the world is potential, and this is nowhere more true than in leadership. It's one thing to understand the problem and another thing entirely to get up and use the abilities and opportunities given to you by God to lead others.

The challenge is that the moment we decide to act, every reason in the world not to comes flooding into our minds. If you are going to move beyond talk, you must deal with the obstacles quickly so that they don't keep you from leading.

One of the most inspiring stories in the Bible is found in the book of Nehemiah. Nehemiah was a man who had a deep love for God and for God's people. At the beginning of the story we find him distraught with the condition of his hometown, Jerusalem. He and many from the nation of Israel had been taken from their homes as captives of the Babylonian empire. Although he was essentially a slave, Nehemiah rose to a place of influence in the court of the king,

Artaxerxes, serving as his butler. Despite his lowly position, he was both trusted and respected by the king. Nehemiah was not going to allow his situation to determine his effectiveness.

It was common in his day for people to get news updates from travelers and merchants from other places, and during a conversation with one of these travelers Nehemiah heard about the condition of Jerusalem. He was told that it was in complete disrepair and that the walls were broken down and the gates to this once great city were burned. He knew he had to do something, but without a clear understanding of what that was, he prayed to God for direction and favor. He received both. The king, a man without a reason to care about his butler, had developed so much respect for Nehemiah that he not only sent him back to Jerusalem to repair the walls, but gave him all the building materials he would need!

So, Nehemiah got to work. He traveled to the king's forest to get the lumber he needed. He organized the project once he arrived in Jerusalem and mobilized the people to do the work. Because of his work, the rebuilding of the walls and city was finished in an incredible 52 days! It would be impossible to get a permit for a wall in 52 days today, but they pulled it off. This was an amazing feat led by an amazing man.

But it was not without its difficulties. Before the incredible work could be finished, certain obstacles had to be dealt with. Enemies of the Jews wanted to keep the work from happening, and scoffers said it would never happen. Some mockingly said that the completed wall would be so weak that it would fall over if a fox even leaned against it.

But Nehemiah didn't seem to care what others thought. He was there to do a job, and they weren't going to stop him. His companions, however, needed to be reminded why they were doing what they were doing. Nehemiah had to encourage them to stop thinking about the project, stop discussing the many difficulties they were encountering, and just get to work. What I love about this passage is that Nehemiah did not motivate them by ridiculing, manipulating, or yelling. He motivated them to get to work by telling them three things that we all need to hear. It was as if he was saying, "Let me tell you why now, with enemies all around, is the time to get busy."

His exact words are,

And I looked, and rose up, and said unto the nobles, and to the rulers, and to the rest of the people, Be not ye afraid of them: remember the Lord, which is great and terrible, and fight for your brethren, your sons, and your daughters, your wives, and your houses (4:14).

The first thing he said was, "Don't be afraid of your enemies." If you read the whole passage, you'll see that he is saying this as their enemies stood mocking and threatening. This was not a theoretical enemy that Nehemiah was talking about. He literally turned his back on the enemies to address the people who were supposed to be doing the work. He understood exactly what they were dealing with, the fear that was keeping them from working, and told them not to let that fear and their very real enemies keep them from fulfilling their purpose.

I love that he starts this way because, whether we like to admit it or not, one of the reasons we don't lead the way we were created to lead is because of fear. We fear attempting something and then failing. We fear being mocked and misunderstood. We fear the hard work and difficulty along with the potential heartache and pain that can come when we step outside of ourselves and *take people from where they are to where they need to be*. Failure, mockery, difficulty, and heartache are all very real enemies that can cause so much fear that we decide leading is just not worth it.

When these enemies present themselves and the fear begins to grow, do what Nehemiah did. Acknowledge their presence. Refuse to let them stop you. Nehemiah didn't pretend that everything was okay, and neither should you. He knew that it looked bad but believed that the work was more important than the obstacles. Don't let what might happen keep you from doing what must happen!

Nehemiah followed up the first statement with a powerful second. He said, "Remember the Lord, which is great and terrible." I can hear the crowd respond to Nehemiah's first statement with something like, "But Nehemiah, how can we possibly deal with the enemies and finish such an enormous project?" It's easy for someone to tell you not to be afraid, but it's harder for them to come up with a good reason not to be afraid, especially amidst an angry mob. But Nehemiah didn't say, "Because of the Lord you should continue the work." He told them to remember the Lord. Those are two very different statements.

Nehemiah was telling them to stop long enough to consider the good things that God had already done in their lives and in their nation. He was telling them to remember how God had delivered the nation of Israel out of captivity in Egypt, how God had parted the Red Sea as they fled the Egyptian army so they could cross in safety. They needed to remember how God had provided food and water for them in the desert and how He had vanquished their enemies in the promised land. They needed to remember how a young man with a sling defeated a giant and how that same young man became the king of their nation. They needed to remember that time and time again throughout their history, the Lord, "great and terrible," had worked through them to do the impossible.

JEREMY STALNECKER

Of course, they had enemies, and clearly the work at hand was bigger than them. Nehemiah was not a motivational speaker who tried to convince them that if they believed hard enough, it would be all right. He was a man who believed that the same God who had worked on Israel's behalf in the past was going to work again.

And that is the point for anyone looking down the road of leadership. It will be hard, and the obstacles and enemies will be many. It may even appear that no amount of effort could possibly change the current situation. This is when leadership is needed most! If things were in order, leadership would be unnecessary. But you don't have to pretend that a situation isn't bad or hope that it'll work out if you believe hard enough. You need to put your faith in a God who has repeatedly demonstrated His faithfulness to accomplish the work He wants done. Your job is to lead where you are, and God's job is to bring the victory. We need to step back and declare as Paul did,

But thanks be to God, which giveth us the victory through our Lord Jesus Christ. 58 Therefore, my beloved brethren, be ye steadfast, unmovable, always abounding in the work of the Lord, forasmuch as ye know that your labour is not in vain in the Lord (First Corinthians 15:57-58).

Finally, Nehemiah proclaimed that now was the time to act because the workers had something worth fighting for. *"Fight for your brethren, your sons, and your daughters, your wives, and your houses."* He reminded them what was at stake if they didn't do what they knew they should do.

Now is the time. There will always be good reasons to play it safe and let others deal with the ups and downs of leadership. If we are willing to pause long enough to really consider what is at stake, though, we will realize that life is too short and the consequences too great for us to sit on the sidelines and let things happen around us. We must stand up and do the thing for which we were created, and now is the time to get started.

There comes a time in all our lives when we need to stop talking and start doing. We need to stop talking about the past and allowing it to define us. We need to stop talking about all that is broken in our world and pointing out those we think are to blame. We need to stop theorizing and planning and understand that there is too much at stake to not do all we can to *take those around us from where they are to where they need to be.* Now is the time. *What are you going to do?*

Discussion Questions

1. What are some things that are keeping you from becoming the leader you were created to be?

2. Why do we often find more comfort in planning and talking than in actually doing?

3. Name some of the "enemies" in your life that keep you from moving forward.

4. Describe some times in your life when God has worked on your behalf.

5. What do you have in your life that is worth fighting for?

Appendix A

What if I don't believe?

> *"Now faith is the substance of things hoped for, the evidence of things not seen."*
>
> **Hebrews 11:1**

Thousands of people have been impacted through the work of Mighty Oaks. Not only do veterans and their spouses attend our programs, but hundreds of active-duty personal from every branch of service attend as well. Add to that the resiliency training we've done at places like Marine Corps Recruit Depot and other active duty commands, and it's safe to say that we have spoken to people from nearly every background and walk of life.

As a faith-based organization we have been asked hundreds of times, "Can I get something out of this if I don't believe?" I understand the heart of the question, but I'm not sure it's entirely accurate. We all believe in something. What that person is really asking is whether they can be helped if they don't believe in God like we do. They want to know if they can take the tools but leave out the "God." Many of the people who attend our programs have tried everything else and have nowhere else to go, so they are willing to try if they don't have to convert.

We do hold a faith-based position, of course, but we have never kept anyone from participating in one of our programs because of their religious background or lack of one. We have had Christians, Buddhists, Universalists, Atheists, Agnostics, and, I am sure, every other shade and dimension on the religious spectrum. We do not change our message, nor do we require some kind of conversion. We just ask for an open mind and an open heart and present the truth as we understand it. Some just take the tools without the faith; others decide they need to put their faith in God through Christ. Still others leave with some answers and a lot of questions that they will process over a lifetime. Our goal is to present the truth that leads to healing so that those who hear can decide what they are going to do with that truth.

I have approached the principles taught in this book the same way we approach our programs. To the best of my ability I have presented what I believe to be true and have tried to motivate the reader to respond to that truth in a way that will allow them to live according to their design. I hope, though, that people who already believe are not the only ones reading this. I hope, as with our programs, that in addition to Christians there are readers whose beliefs fall all over the religious spectrum as well as those who would say that they have no faith at all. The question, then, is, "What if I don't believe?"

When the premise is that we were created to lead and that we understand leadership from the perspective of creation, belief becomes very important. *So for those who do not share my worldview, is there hope and direction to be found in a book like this?* I will address this with one final story and a few closing points.

The Story

As I mentioned earlier, I had the privilege of serving with First Battalion Fifth Marines during the initial invasion into Iraq. It was a privilege, not because war is something to honor, but because it was an honor serving with some of the best men I have ever known during a significant moment in world history. As we sat south of the border during the weeks leading up to the invasion, though, the long days were often difficult to deal with. Looking back, I think it was all part of the plan. We were so bored that by the time we could move into Iraq we were just excited to do something! You can only play so many games of cards before you begin to lose your mind.

As I was walking toward our battalion command post on one of these days, I happened to cross paths with the Fifth Marine Regiment Commanding Officer, Colonel Joe Dunford. That was fourteen years ago, and Colonel Dunford is now General Dunford and the head of the Joint Chiefs of Staff. He was then, as he is now, an incredible leader who had better things to do than stop and talk to a lieutenant. But that day, he did.

I offered him the appropriate greeting and, much to my surprise, he stopped me to talk about the overall morale and preparation of the Marines. As a lieutenant I knew that the only right answer was that everything was great and the Marines just couldn't wait to get going. He then took about thirty seconds to tell me everything that was in place to make our movement into Iraq as smooth and safe as possible. He said that it was his goal to hit the enemy so hard before we even got there with air power and artillery that they wouldn't want to fight. Because I don't know when to keep my mouth shut, I asked him to leave us something to do because that's what we'd been training for! He told me to make sure I kept my Marines ready and walked away.

I didn't think about it then, but I have since learned a great leadership lesson from that conversation. The regimental commander did not stop and talk to a lieutenant to discuss morale or even the strategic war plan. Because he understood leadership, he wanted to communicate to his men at every level, including the bottom level where I operated, that he was going to take care of us. He knew that I would tell others about our interaction and that, hopefully, confidence in him and in the process would increase because he had made a promise to a smart aleck lieutenant that none of us could actually make him keep.

When the war started a couple of weeks later and my unit pushed toward the border, I will never forget looking out the window into the night sky and seeing what looked like a firework display. I was seeing thousands of artillery rounds being fired on our first objective so that the enemy wouldn't want to fight when we got there. At that moment, I realized that Colonel Dunford had kept his word. There were still guys on the other side of the border who wanted to fight, but most of those first few days were spent collecting soldiers who had given up without a fight because the opening barrage was so bad.

Final Thoughts

While I know that human examples have a hard time illustrating something as big as faith in an infinite God, they do provide a helpful picture. As I consider the story above, a few relevant points come to mind.

1. Truth is true whether I believe it or not. Colonel Dunford made a statement that was true. He knew what was going to happen when the war started and that we would not move to the border unless it happened. Whether I believed him was irrelevant and had no bearing on whether what he told me was true. He never even asked me if I believed him. This was a statement of fact and not a point of discussion.

2. Truth impacts everyone, not just those who believe. Anyone who has spent time around Marines will tell you that every Marine believes no one with a rank higher than the one they wear has any idea what they're doing. Everyone, it seems, is an idiot. But even those who believed that their higher-ups had no idea what they were doing benefited from the plan that was in place to greatly limit the ability of the enemy. Disbelief did not change the truth or the outcome. On the other side of this I have often wondered what the Iraqi army thought when those artillery rounds began hitting the ground. They had been told, and many believed, that the United States would never be able to cross the border into their country. But it still happened. Their lack of belief did not change the truth.

3. The source of truth is important. When Colonel Dunford told me that everything was going to be okay, I had no reason to doubt him. I had never seen him do what he said he would do, and truthfully, he had never done it. But the available evidence was a strong indication that I should believe. I had been part of large training exercises led by his staff that included all the elements he said would be present during the first days of the war. I had read his plan and watched him explain it to the regiment's staff and officers. I had never heard him say he would do something that he did not follow through on. If I looked at his statement and decided whether to believe it simply based on the evidence I had available to me, I couldn't help but believe. He had already demonstrated an ability and willingness to keep his word.

Even if you don't agree with the premise of this book (the premise of creation), you can still benefit from the principles because truth impacts everyone including those who don't believe. If the principles are true, then a consistent application will bring about consistent outcomes. Some will dismiss these principles because they think truth is relative and what is true for some is not true for others. Truth is true whether you believe it or not. Truth does not work for some and not work for others. If it is true, then even a lack of belief will not keep the truth, if consistently applied, from doing its work. A lack of belief has no bearing on the potential impact of truth.

The source of truth, however, is important. Not everything that claims to be true really is, and only by honestly examining the available evidence can we draw an accurate conclusion. It is the same with truth taken from the Bible. Belief in the Bible is something we call faith, but faith, contrary to what many believe, is not closed-minded acceptance. It is believing based on an examination of the evidence. Hebrews 11:1 says, *"Now faith is the substance of things hoped for, the evidence of things not seen."* Not everything that claims to be true is, but it is reasonable to conclude based on the mountain of evidence available to us that God's words can be trusted. He has demonstrated throughout time his ability to do what He says He will do and that He is a trustworthy source when considering our design.

Can you benefit from the principles taught here if they come from God, even if you don't believe? If these principles are faithfully and consistently applied, you will be a better leader for having applied them.

So why is belief important, if unnecessary, for the principles to be effective? In one word—confidence. As the early part of the war dragged on it felt like rest of any kind was nothing but a distant memory. We would stay awake for days at a time moving to the next objective on the list. We would hear that the next town or objective would be a bad one but that it wouldn't matter because we would run out of food and water before we got there anyway. And yet we pressed on. As overwhelming as some of those moments were, I don't remember a time when I felt like it wasn't going to be okay. I had confidence in those who were making the big decisions, which continued to give me hope even when things were at their worst.

As leaders, it is one thing to adopt principles that work but quite another thing to have confidence that they will work even when the circumstances around us seem to be out of control. Belief is important because it gives us the confidence to live according to our design and know that things will turn out exactly as they should. Consider the source, examine the evidence, and move forward confidently, living according to your design.

For the person who is still unsure, I end with this. If you look at the evidence and there is still something keeping you from putting your confidence in the Creator, begin living and leading by the principles He has given and see where it takes you. I am never afraid of where a person will end up if they are willing to honestly examine the evidence available to them and live their life according to it. Life and faith are a journey. Start where you are and you will be amazed where the road will take you.

Appendix B
A Relationship with the Creator

> *"Therefore if any man be in Christ, he is a new creature: old things are passed away; behold, all things are become new."*
> **- Second Corinthians 5:17**

Many of you already have a relationship with God through His Son Jesus Christ. You have experienced the forgiveness of sins and the new life found when we surrender to the will of our Creator. It is an amazing thing to know that the One who created the universe and all it contains would desire to have a personal relationship with each one of us. Followers of Christ are far from perfect, but they have the ability to recognize their imperfection and rest in the One who gives them life. To be fully what we were created to be is not possible without this personal relationship. If you have accepted God's gift of salvation, you have all that you need to apply these principles of leadership and be the leader you were created to be.

Others reading this have not yet entered into that personal relationship. For one reason or another you have not accepted that you can or should align yourself with God's eternal purpose for you. There are many reasons that people do not accept this gift. If you are reading this, you are clearly not averse to the Christian worldview. Perhaps you've been hurt or disillusioned by the behavior of those who call themselves Christians or are simply, and honestly, trying to make the best decision. Whatever the case, I cannot end this book without telling you how to have that relationship.

Having a relationship with God is about so much more than leadership, but without that relationship you can never truly be all that you were created to be both in leadership and in life. God created us to be perfect. There was no brokenness in the beginning, and we were in complete communion with Him. We are even told in the third chapter of Genesis that God would personally spend time each evening with the first humans.

But then mankind, through our common father Adam, decided to rebel against God's will and do what He had expressly told them not to do. This disobedience (what we call sin) broke our perfect relationship with God and made it impossible for man to walk in communion with Him. Because of sin, this broken relationship carries with it a penalty—separation from God forever in a place called Hell. Certainly not something we like to talk about, but a reality that we all must face.

The great light in this dark story is that God still wants to have a relationship with us and has made that possible through His Son, Jesus Christ. By accepting His gift of forgiveness of sins, each of us can be forgiven and given a new life through Him. Our relationship and communion with the Creator will be restored and our life will be in line with His purpose.

Having a relationship with Christ and experiencing forgiveness of sins is not some formulaic process but rather an acceptance of a gift freely offered to us by Him. Some thoughts for those who would like to enter in to that relationship:

1. Recognize your condition.

To find the way to eternal life with God, you must admit that you are lost in sin. Romans 5:12 teaches us that since Adam and Eve, the first man and woman on earth, a sin nature has been present in all people. Romans 3:23 says, *"For all have sinned, and come short of the glory of God."* Sin is any act contrary to God's laws and commandments, and the sins I have committed separate me from God. Sin has a penalty. Romans 6:23 says, *"For the wages of sin is death; but the gift of God is eternal life through Jesus Christ our Lord."* The wage or payment for our sin is spiritual death and eternal separation from God.

2. Realize that religion and good works are not the answer.

Religions try to create their own ways to God. Their systems may seem logical, but they cannot bridge the gap created by our sin. Proverbs 14:12 says, *"There is a way which seemeth right unto a man, but the end thereof are the ways of death."* In other words, our thoughts and ways are not what matter. God's Word, the Bible, provides true answers of grace and forgiveness. In Ephesians 2:8–9 the Bible says, *"For by grace are ye saved through faith; and that not of yourselves: it is the gift of God: Not of works, lest any man should boast."*

3. The good news is that Jesus has made a way!

Even though we were lost and separated from God, He loved us. Because of that love, God sent His Son to die on the cross and raised him from the dead three days later. John 3:16 explains *"For God so loved the world, that he gave his only begotten Son, that whosoever believeth in him should not perish, but have everlasting life."* Through the death and resurrection of Jesus, He became the payment for our sin. Now we do not have to pay for our sin ourselves. By His grace, salvation is provided. Romans 5:8 says, *"But God commendeth* [meaning proved or demonstrated] *his love toward us, in that, while we were yet sinners, Christ died for us."*

4. Believe and receive Christ.

In order to have a relationship with God and an eternal home in Heaven, we must stop trusting ourselves, our works, and our religions, and place our full trust in Jesus Christ alone for the forgiveness of our sin and eternal life. Roman 10:13 says, *"For whosoever shall call upon the name of the Lord shall be saved."* That is a promise directly from God that if you will pray to Him, confess that you are a sinner, ask Him to forgive your sins, and turn to Him alone to be your Savior, He promises to save you and give you the free gift of eternal life. You can make that decision by praying to Him today.

There are no magic words and no magic prayers. God simply desires to hear you express an understanding of your need for Him and your desire to have a relationship with Him. My prayer is that if you have not yet entered into that relationship, today is the day you accept His gift of salvation and begin living in relationship with your Creator.

Appendix C
Additional Resources

"Not all readers are leaders, but all leaders are readers."

– Harry S. Truman

While I have done my best throughout the preceding pages to convey the "heart" of leadership, I have done very little to provide the practical steps of leadership that need to be coupled with that heart. I firmly believe that if the heart or philosophy of leadership are right that the practical steps will follow. I also understand that we can all use direction at times and much has been written on this topic that has been extremely helpful in my own life as I have sought to lead in a way that reflects who God created me to be. To that end, I have put together the following list. This is not a comprehensive list of books on leadership, but is a good start for anyone that hopes to lead to their full, God-given potential.

Spiritual Leadership Principles

Spiritual Leadership, J. Oswald Sanders

Spiritual Leadership, Henry Blackaby

Disciplines of a Godly Man, Kent Hughes

On Being a Servant of God, Warren Wiersbe

Lead Like Jesus, Ken Blanchard and Phil Hodges

The Disciplined Life, Richard Taylor

General Leadership Principles

The 21 Irrefutable Laws of Leadership, John Maxwell

Developing the Leader Within You, John Maxwell

Working with Emotional Intelligence, Daniel Goleman

Good to Great, Jim Collins

Team of Rivals, Doris Kearns Goodwin

Man's Search for Meaning, Viktor Frankl

The Seven Habits of Highly Effective People, Stephen Covey

Tribes, Seth Godin

How to Win Friends and Influence People, Dale Carnegie

The War of Art, Steven Pressfield

About the Author

Jeremy M. Stalnecker

Executive Director,

Mighty Oaks Foundation

Former USMC Infantry Officer

Pastor

Jeremy Stalnecker is the Executive Director of the Mighty Oaks Foundation. The Mighty Oaks Foundation is dedicated to helping America's military warriors and their families who are suffering from the unseen wounds of combat such as Post Traumatic Stress Disorder (PTSD).

JEREMY STALNECKER

While growing up in San Jacinto, CA, Jeremy's only goal in life was to leave home and join the Marine Corps. This dream was finally realized with an active duty commission in 1999. Following Infantry Officer Course in Quantico, VA, Jeremy was assigned to First Battalion, Fifth Marines, First Marine Division as an infantry platoon commander. Serving first as a rifle platoon commander in a helicopter company and then as the platoon commander of the counter-mechanized platoon, Jeremy learned valuable leadership and communication skills that he continues to use today. In January 2003, Fifth Marines, as a part of the First Marine Division, deployed to Kuwait in support of what would become Operation Iraqi Freedom. As the war began, First Battalion, Fifth Marines was the infantry battalion used to breech the berm separating Kuwait and Iraq and secured the first major objective of the war. This led to a road march that ended with the battalion occupying Baghdad and seizing the presidential palace in northern Baghdad on the Tigris River. Throughout this movement, Jeremy and the counter-mechanized platoon provided navigation and lead security for the battalion.

While in the Marine Corps, God was working in Jeremy's life to turn his heart toward full-time ministry. Just one month after returning from Iraq, Jeremy became a staff member of his home church at Coastline Baptist in Oceanside, CA. Here he gained ministry experience that would equip him for the further leading of God. In his role as an Assistant Pastor, he counseled and mentored many couples and individuals while also maintaining other church responsibilities. It was a great privilege for him to be able to serve in this capacity so close to Camp Pendleton since most of the people he worked with were either Marines or the family members of Marines.

In 2008, Jeremy and his family took on a new responsibility when he became the Senior Pastor, just east of San Francisco Bay at Bay Area Baptist Church in Fremont, CA. In this capacity, he continued to minister to families and individuals in a wide range of areas. After serving in the role of senior pastor for nearly seven years, the door leading to a full-time position with the Mighty Oaks Foundation opened. This move brought together both his ministry experience and military background in a way that allows him to serve and minister to many hurting veterans, service members and their families. Along with his wife Susanne and their four children, Jeremy works to reach the hurting and provide the healing found in Christ.

Endotes

1   ZIg Ziglar, Power Quotations, www.powerquotations.com

2   "Operation Cobra," https://en.wikipedia.org

3   Elizabeth McLaughlin, VA Releases Results of Largest Analysis of Veteran Suicide Rates, www.abcnews.go.com, July 2016

4   100 Best Quotes on Leadership, www.forbes.com

5   Ibid.

6   The Titanic Page, www.eszlinger.com

7   Ibid.

8   Ibid.

9   Titanic: 40 Fascinating Facts, www.telegraph.co.uk

10 Ibid.

11 10 Lesser-Known Facts About the Titanic, www.listverse.com

12 Shiza Shahid, Lack of Leadership, www.reports.weforum.org

13 Mike Hyatt, Business Don't Fail, Leaders Do, www.forbes.com, January 2012

14 U.S. Public Becoming Less Religious, www.pewforum.org

15 Thom Rainer, The Most Common Factor in Declining Churches, www.lifeway.com, August 2016

16 Pogo, www.en.wikipedia.org

17 Theodore Roosevelt, www.theodore-roosevelt.com

18 C.S. Lewis, The Weight of Glory, 1941

19 Art Lindsley, Made in the Image of God-The basis for Our Significance, tifwe.org

20 William Shakespear, Molvolio, www.en.wikipedia.org

21 Dick Staub, www.relevantmagazine.com

22 www.dictionary.com

23 J.P. Moreland, Love Your God With All Your Mind, (Colorado Springs, NavPress, 1997)

24 Martin Luther King Jr., I have a dream, www.americanrhetoric.com

25 Harvey Deutschendorf, Emotional Intelligence and Lincoln: 5 Leadership Principles,www.business2community.com

26 www.dictionary.com

27 Fox's Book of Martyrs, www.ccel.org

28 Spiros Zodhiates, The Complete Word Study Dictionary (AMG International, 1992), pg 252

29 Zodhiates, The Complete Word Study Dictionary, pg 378

30 Ibid., pg 500

31 Ibid., pg 1425

32 New Englands Dark Day, www.en.wikipedia.org

33 Zodhiates, The Complete Word Study Dictionary, pg 683

34 Ibid., pg 1444

35 Ibid., pg 66

36 Abraham Lincoln, Abraham Lincolns Lyceum Address, en.wikipedia. org

37 www.quotes.lifehack.org

38 Kent Hughes, Disciplines of a Godly Man, Crossway Books, Wheaton Ill, 2001

39 John Powell, Why am I afraid to tell you who I am, Zondervan Grand Rapids, MI 1999

40 www.thinkexist.com

41 Daniel Burnham, www.en.wikiquote.org

42 U.S. Census Bureau, Children's Living Arrangements and Characteristics: March 2011, Table C8. Washington D.C.: 2011

43 Hofferth, S. L. (2006). Residential father family type and child well-being: investment versus selection. Demography, 43, 53-78

44 Edward Kruk, Ph.D., "The Vital Importance of Paternal Presence in Children's Lives." May 23, 2012

45 Knoester, C., & Hayne, D.A. (2005). "Community context, social integration into family, and youth violence." Journal of Marriage and Family 67, 767-780

46 Bush, Connee, Ronald L. Mullis, and Ann K. Mullis. "Differences in Empathy Between Offender and Nonoffender Youth." Journal of Youth and Adolescence 29 (August 2000): 467-478

47 Hopkinsmedicine.org, April 2010

48 C.S. Lewis, The Screwtape Letters, Geoffrey Bles, 1942

49 Billy Montana and Steve Dean, The Preacher Won't have to Lie, 1998

50 Robert Lewis, The Heart of Manhood, www.christianitytoday.com

51 Abraham Lincoln, www.abrahamlincolnonline.org

JEREMY STALNECKER SPEAKING ENGAGEMENTS

Jeremy delivers powerful presentations to various audiences including:

- **CORPORATE OUTINGS**
- **CHURCH SERVICES & EVENTS**
- **MILITARY EVENTS**
- **RESILIENCY CONFERENCES**
- **MEN'S EVENTS**

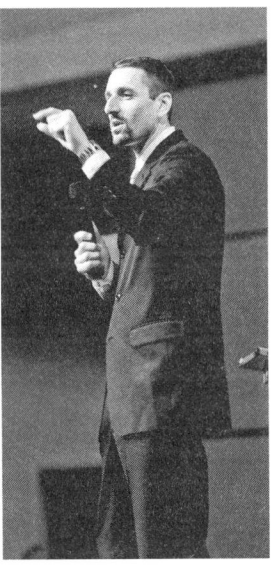

Jeremy has a passion to share his transformational experiences, as well as those he has witnessed from the Warriors he leads through the Mighty Oaks Warrior Programs.

Jeremy's presentations on the following topics are both inspiring and challenging and can be scaled from single sessions to multi-day/multi-session retreats and conferences:

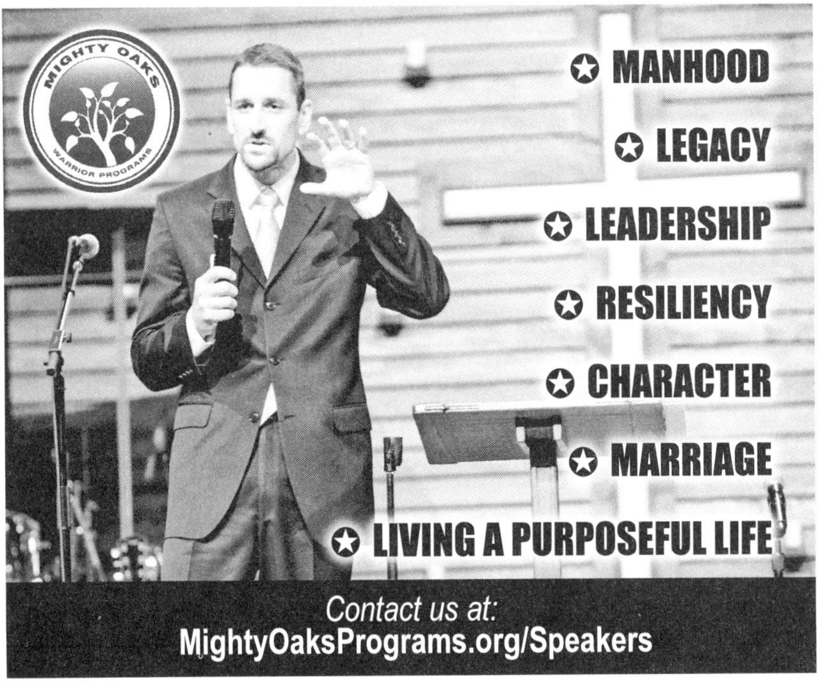
MIGHTY OAKS
WARRIOR PROGRAMS
MANHOOD
LEGACY
LEADERSHIP
RESILIENCY
CHARACTER
MARRIAGE
LIVING A PURPOSEFUL LIFE

Contact us at:
MightyOaksPrograms.org/Speakers

MIGHTY OAKS WARRIOR PROGRAMS

LEGACY PROGRAM FOR MEN - Our six-day intensive peer to peer program serves as the catalyst to help Warriors discover the answers to the big questions in life. Challenges related to the struggles of daily military life, combat deployments and the symptoms of post-traumatic stress (PTS) surface during these six days, and the Legacy Program for Men teaches how to fight through these challenges, which might have been limiting their personal success.

LEGACY PROGRAM FOR WOMEN - The Legacy Program for Women is a process of learning to become a Virtuous Woman – "The Proverbs 31" woman. This three-day retreat leads spouses and military women through a time of learning, exploration and growth with an aim to cultivate virtuous characteristics in a safe, open, nurturing environment.

MARRIAGE ADVANCE: LOVE NEVER GIVES UP - Our three day Marriage Advance Program is designed for couples to gain a better understanding of the struggles they each face. We structure conversations around needs, expectations, goals and forgiveness to help couples move forward.

MILITARY RESILIENCY PROGRAMS - We believe that *"Resiliency"* is comprised of three pillars: *mind, body and spirit.* Our Military Resiliency Programs are designed to properly equip our nation's Warriors on the front end of conflict, so they and their families can have a true *"Resiliency"* and a mindset that is preventative of the hardships that many of them face.

These programs are NO cost to our Warriors.
To support or learn more please visit:

www.MightyOaksPrograms.org

An official program of Mighty Oaks Foundation, a 501c3 Non-Profit Organization

OTHER MIGHTY OAKS RESOURCES

✪ An Unfair Advantage ✪
By Chad Robichaux

Take a journey with Force Recon Marine and Pro Mixed Martial Arts Champion Fighter, Chad Robichaux, as he shares a glimpse into the life of special operations, competition as a professional fighter, and the deep insight into this world's spiritual battles which we are all engaged. Chad shares personal stories of both success and failure experienced in Afghanistan, the MMA cage, and his biggest fight of all... coming home and facing a struggle with PTSD, a near divorce and almost becoming another veteran suicide statistic. Each chapter shares a parallel story of Biblical-time warriors who faced similar struggles and reveals *An Unfair Advantage* that led them to victory in the midst of those battles. Discover that same advantage for the battles you face and unlock the warrior spirit sewn in your heart by God Himself.

✪ Path to Resiliency ✪
By Chad Robichaux & Jeremy Stalnecker

This book was written to challenge the greatest of Warriors, whether military or civilian, man or woman... to be ready for, resilient to, and able to reintegrate from life's trials and rigors. You don't have to go to Iraq or Afghanistan to face the hardships and trials of life! Military service member or not, we all find ourselves in moments of adversity and hardship from time to time. When we do, will you have the resiliency to overcome.

✪ Marriage Advance ✪
Love Never Gives Up
By: Chad and Kathy Robichaux
*(26 week testimonial based marriage
workbook for couples)*

Struggling against the odds can be difficult. It is always easier to give up and surrender than to endure the hardships that come with holding on. But success can only come to those who find the fortitude to stay in the fight. When you give up, there is no chance of success.

Join Chad and Kathy Robichaux as they lead you through 26 weeks of compelling stories with practical questions, helping you build a stronger marriage that will always be "advancing" toward the ultimate success God had in mind when YOU said, "I DO!"

THE **MIGHTY OAKS** PODCAST
★ ★ ★

with **CHAD** ROBICHAUX **&** **JEREMY** STALNECKER | *Finding Victory in Life's Battles*

TUNE IN EVERY FRIDAY 10am PST
Subscribe Now! www.TheMightyOaksPodcast.com

See these resources on the "STORE" page at:
www.MightyOaksPrograms.org